BLUEPRINT

for Success

POWERHOUSE PROFESSIONALS

14

INSIGHT PUBLISHING
SEVIERVILLE, TENNESSEE

Table of Contents

A Message from the Publisher...

When we see the word "blueprint" we usually think of a technical drawing or other image rendered as white lines on a blue background produced by an architect. A blueprint is a detailed plan of action and everyone should develop a blueprint in order to plan for success in life. The men and women in this book have, in interesting and innovative ways, developed their own blueprints that paved the way for their success.

As I interviewed these people, I found that there are as many ways to plan for success as there are people who create those plans. I was fascinated as I learned from these highly successful people what they did to succeed in their various professions. A successful businesswoman once told me that when she was "involuntarily separated from her last corporate job" she took the opportunity to sit back and take a deep breath, discover what she really wanted to do, and to explore her passion. She said she didn't write anything down but from just taking some time out to think and explore, she came up with her path to success.

At times, successful people have to push through hard times and setbacks. I am always intrigued by the various methods they use to overcome difficulties. Some of them have gone on to teach others what they learned as they went back to the drawing board and created a new blueprint that led them to success.

I believe you will find that your time will be well spent in reading this book. I think you will find that these people have something to say that is worth listening to. I know that I did.

Interviews Conducted by:
David E. Wright, President
International Speakers Network

Chapter One

An interview with...

Tim Kelley

David Wright (Wright)
Today we're talking with Tim Kelley, who has helped thousands of people find their life's purpose. He is a celebrated speaker and best-selling author.
Tim, welcome to *Blueprint for Success!*

Tim Kelley (Kelley)
Thank you very much, David!

Wright
What is a "life purpose?"

Kelley
Each of us has a unique life purpose—some reason why we are here— someone we are meant to be, and something we are meant to do. Not everyone believes this, but the people who *do* believe it often get an itch, a feeling, or a calling. They have a sense that there is something they are supposed to be doing, and until they are doing it they don't feel completely fulfilled in their lives. From my point of view, it's a question that each of us needs to answer, because we'll be happier, more successful, and more fulfilled when we do.

Wright
Why would I want to find my life's purpose?

Kelley
Imagine that there's something that you've been meant to do all along, and you've been designed for it and trained for it your whole life. If that's the case, it would follow that you'd be very good at that thing. You can use a

hammer to drive screws, but it's really designed for driving nails. Unless you're driving nails with it, it's going to seem like it's not really doing its best work. People do their best work when they're doing their purpose, and as a result they tend to be happier and more fulfilled and their lives have more meaning—and often they make more money as well. People who set out to "make money" often wind up being unhappy as a result, but people who set out to find and fulfill their purpose tend to lead happier, more fulfilled lives. People are usually paid better when they're doing something at which they're amazing.

Wright

That makes sense! What prevents people from finding their purpose?

Kelley

Except in very rare cases, every person will have fears and reservations about finding his or her purpose. Those fears can look a lot of different ways: "What would happen if I found my purpose? What might go wrong? What would my spouse think? What would my boss think? Would I have to change jobs? Would I be able to make money at my purpose? Would I have to move? What would society think of me? Would I have to go to another country and help starving people?" There are all kinds of fears and concerns people have about their purpose. Some of the fears come from the belief that if it *is* your purpose, then you *have* to do it—and that's not actually true.

These fears and concerns keep the part of us that knows our purpose— the voice in us that already has the answers—very quiet. The fears and concerns drown it out. People's universal state seems to be that they have some desire to know their purpose, some fears about knowing their purpose, and therefore their understanding of their purpose stays very vague.

Wright

So what do I do about these fears?

Kelley

What you can't do is override them. You can't tough it out and say, "I'm concerned that if I find my purpose I might not make money at it, but I'm going to ignore that fear and go ahead anyway."

There are several different ways of getting through these fears and obstacles. One of them is actually to talk to the parts of you that are having the fears. This usually requires outside help from someone like a hypnotherapist, a neurolinguistic programming (NLP) practitioner, or a Voice Dialogue facilitator. More commonly, this can be done through a journaling process: sit down and list all the different fears you have about finding your purpose. Then take one of the fears, say it's the fear about money. Ask yourself, "What would happen if I found my purpose and I couldn't make enough money doing it?" So what's the worst thing that could happen? "I wouldn't be able to pay my mortgage." Great, write that down. Then what? "Then my family would be out on the street." Keep doing it—for each thing you think of, write down something worse. Eventually you can't think of anything worse. And once you have the worst-case scenario, ask yourself, "If all these bad things happened would I still pursue my purpose?" For some people the answer is "yes," it's that important to them; they would go for it even if they thought it was going to result in all these terrible things.

In other cases, people would say, "Well, no, of course not! I *have* to feed my family. If I weren't making enough money and it would put my family on the street, I would stop pursuing my purpose and find some other way to make money."

Interestingly, that doesn't prevent you from finding your purpose. It reassures you that you won't do anything crazy once you've found it. You won't hurt yourself or the people around you or make yourself look bad. You won't make any stupid decisions just because you know your purpose. And if you go through this process thoroughly, taking each fear to its worst possible case, then it becomes safe to find your purpose. You don't have to worry about what it is. You'll find your purpose, and if it's something that you don't like or don't want to do, you won't do it! If you don't go through this process—carefully exploring each and every fear—then it's nearly impossible to find your purpose.

Wright

I have a daughter I just sent off to college who hasn't declared her major. I'm glad of that because she is trying to deal with finding her purpose—what is she supposed to be doing? That doesn't mean finding what will make the most money, but what would best fit her. What kind of advice would you give someone like her?

Kelley

"What is my purpose" is a tough question to answer when you're that young. The training phase of life usually takes anywhere from thirty to sixty years, meaning that you're out there doing the best that you can, trying on all sorts of different things, taking jobs, going to school, having relationships, and bumping and grinding your way through life. From the point of view of the part of you that already knows your purpose, that's just training—you are learning to become an instrument of your purpose. And until that training phase is nearly complete, there's not that much value in learning the details of your purpose. It would be just a distraction. So the part of you that knows your purpose tends to withhold that information, usually until you are at least in your late thirties, although that age limit seems to be dropping lately. It seems that more and more young people are actually finding their purpose; but traditionally it was people in their forties, fifties, and sixties who would find it.

But until you've completed that training phase and really put your attention on your purpose, it's better to keep doing the best you can. Then one day you say, "All right, what is my purpose?" This usually happens at the point we call a midlife crisis, when you realize the things you've been doing may *not* be the most meaningful things in the world. This is when the need for purpose shows up in a big way. It can show up rather dramatically via car accidents, diseases, firings, divorces, and all sorts of things that call your attention to *meaning*—"What is the meaning of my life?" That usually happens much later in life.

Wright

So purpose can be a journey in some cases?

Kelley

Oh yes, it's a journey; it's a life-long process! There's the journey before you know your purpose, and then there's the journey after you know your purpose—but it's still a journey either way. Finding your purpose doesn't remove all the struggle and challenge from your life! Not knowing your purpose is one kind of struggle—not being sure of the right path, trying different things, and being unclear what it's all about. There's struggle when we're doing things that aren't purposeful—drudgery, boredom, lack of meaning, feeling unfulfilled.

Once you know your purpose, then you have to take action on it, and that can be challenging. Many people don't want to know their purpose because they don't want the responsibility or the challenge. But that's the journey—the path worth walking! Having a purpose and being challenged by it is a life filled with growth, fulfillment, and magic.

Wright

Which way of finding your purpose works best?

Kelley

There are two broad categories of methods to find your purpose. I call them "indirect methods" and "direct methods."

Indirect methods are the most popular. When you use indirect methods you try to figure out what your purpose must be based on the available evidence. An example of available evidence is your life to date. If you look at all the different times in your life when you've felt the most passionate, fulfilled, and aligned, they are probably times when you were doing something relatively purposeful. What's the pattern? What's the common thread in those incidents in your life when you really *did* feel connected to your purpose? These types of exercises are very popular; they are taught in coaching schools and you can find them in books. There are other common questions like, what would you do if you had a year to live? Or, what you do if you won the lottery? Or, what do you wish people would say about you at your funeral? There are many different questions like these that elicit purpose information. If you answer a bunch of these questions and then sift through the answers, preferably with the help of a trained coach—it's nearly impossible to do this by yourself—then you will find patterns in your answers. The patterns contain information about your purpose.

The problem with these methods is that they're not terribly accurate. They produce an approximate purpose—it's hard to really "nail it" using an indirect method. But these methods are the most common, mostly because they're so easy to use. If you run across people who say they know their purpose, usually they found it this way—by looking at the available evidence, going back through their lives, and answering purpose-related questions.

The more accurate approach is using what I call "direct methods," which are things like meditation, prayer, sleeping dreams, and certain types of journaling that give you direct access to your purpose. If you believe you already have a purpose, then something or someone must already know what it is. For example, this could mean that your purpose is contained somewhere within you. This gets tricky because where you go looking for your purpose is dependent on your religious or spiritual belief system. It makes these methods much harder to use. For example, if you're a monotheist, such as a Christian, a Muslim, or a Jew, then God knows your purpose. You might also believe that you have a soul, and that your soul knows your purpose. Those would be places you could go to find your purpose. If you were a Christian, you could also talk to Jesus or the Holy Spirit.

If you were a Native American, perhaps your spirit animal guide would know your purpose. If you were a New Age person, perhaps your Higher Self or your guide or Source would know your purpose. Different people view the universe very differently, but in most people's belief system there's something that already knows their purpose, whether it's inside of them or outside of them. I call that thing "a trusted source."

What all the direct access methods have in common is that they create a two-way conversation with a trusted source. This means that you can ask,

"What is my purpose?" When it works, you get a direct answer in words, such as, "Glad you asked. Your purpose is to . . ." When it comes right down to it, it's really that simple and straightforward.

The tough part is what I talked about earlier, clearing a path through the fears and anxiety about your purpose that will allow you to have this conversation. If you haven't dealt with your fears yet, this will not work. If you've dealt with your fears, then you can set up a two-way dialogue using any of the direct methods. You can ask questions and get answers. You can receive very explicit, detailed information about your life's purpose, not the vague information you usually get from the indirect methods.

Wright

So a trusted source, then, would be whatever people think of as their God, their higher power, or whatever?

Kelley

Yes. A trusted source is some entity that already knows your purpose and is capable of communication. So for a religious person, that would be God. The one who created me knows my purpose, and in different religions I might name that being differently. But if it were a person who was *not* religious and *didn't* believe in God, it might be something else like "Source" or "the Universe."

Some people are uncomfortable with a universal divine source of any kind, and are only willing to look inward. In that case, ask yourself, "What part of me knows my purpose?" That could be your soul, your spirit, your Higher Self, or your Buddha nature. It depends upon what language you use to describe that part of yourself.

Whether it's inside of you or outside of you, whatever you call it, if it's something that already knows your purpose and it's capable of communication, then it qualifies as a "trusted source." And as long as you've dealt with your fears, you can talk to it and it can tell you your purpose in great detail.

Wright

So can we break life purpose down? What are the different parts?

Kelley

Life's purpose is a big murky concept, and when different people say "purpose" they mean different things. As I said at the beginning, to me life purpose is why you're here, that is, who you're meant to be and what you're meant to do. This means that there is both a "being" and a "doing" aspect to purpose. If we break down these being and doing aspects further, the question, "What is my life's purpose?" makes much more sense.

For clarity, I break it up into three aspects.

The first is "essence." Essence is the pure being aspect of purpose. It is your purpose when you are standing still, your purpose when you are not doing anything. So at this level you *are* your purpose, rather than you *do* your purpose. Different people have different essences; they radiate from us like light or heat, and they affect the people around us. I can't see or feel my essence, but *you* are affected by it. You're being affected by it right now, and I'm being affected by yours. But you can't see your own essence. Whenever someone walks in a room, everyone in the room is affected by that person's essence, whether he or she is aware of it or not. People have all sorts of different essences, like love or compassion or joy or challenge or enlightenment. There are many, many different essences and each of us has our own. That's the *being* aspect of purpose.

The *doing* aspect of purpose—what you do when you're doing your purpose—I call "blessing." I call it that because you do your purpose to another human being—you "bless" him or her with your purpose. This isn't just an activity or an ability; in fact, it's a *process,* and like any process it has steps. You do the steps and it has an impact on another person, and he or she is changed by it in some way. You bless others, and they are the recipients of your blessing. To really understand this aspect of your purpose, you would have to understand what all those steps are, and you would have to understand to whom you are meant to offer this blessing. You would have to understand what the impact of your blessing is when you do it with the individuals who receive it.

My blessing is to help people find their path. It's intended to be used with lost people, so my best work as a consultant and a coach is done with people and organizations that are trying to find their way; those are the people I've been sent to serve with my blessing. I help them find their way, and I help them decide whether they want to walk the path that's been laid out for them or not. Other people I know create harmony in relationships or help groups ground their attention and then raise their energy up—there are all sorts of different blessings in the world.

There are many, many different ways that one can use a blessing. I've used my blessing to help people find their path as a navigator in the Navy. I've used it as a college interviewer to people leaving high school and making college choices, I've used it helping organizations find their vision and mission, and I've used it helping CEOs find their life's purpose. All of these are different ways of helping people find their path, and all of them have been deeply fulfilling and moving to me. I'm a better person when I'm helping people find their path than when I'm doing anything else.

The third aspect of purpose is something called "mission." Mission is just what it sounds like: "Your mission, should you choose to accept it, is to . . ." You've been sent here with your essence and blessing—tools you've been given to achieve some end in the world. That end is your mission—to accomplish some goal, make some change, solve some problem, or serve some group of people.

Some people don't have a mission. I know people who are just sent to the world to bring love. And to bring love to whom? Everybody, anybody—it doesn't matter. In whatever way they choose to do it, it's fine. These people don't have a mission in the true sense of the word; they are meant to express their blessing in any way they like.

And there are other people for whom the tasking is much more specific: work with *this* group of people, or solve *this* problem. I know a guy whose mission is to solve the world's food and energy problems (big mission!)

My mission is to change business from an ego-driven activity to a purpose-driven activity. I can help many lost people find their path, but my mission is to help leaders find their path because it will create a change in business.

You don't have to accept your mission. Everyone has an essence. You are your essence—you have no choice about it. Everyone has a blessing. You do your blessing in every job and every relationship you've ever had, whether you're aware of it or not—it's usually done unconsciously. But not everyone has a mission, and you can say "no" to your mission if you have one.

Wright

So once I've found my purpose, then what?

Kelley

I'm saying that "purpose = essence + blessing + mission." It's the sum of those three things: your essence, your blessing, and your mission, if you have one. Having found your purpose, then you have some decisions to make. If you used one of the direct methods to talk to your trusted source, and you've been told your purpose, then you have to ask, "How do I feel about that? Do I believe that really was my trusted source talking? Do I believe that this really is my purpose?" There are ways to tell whether the process really worked. Finding your purpose often causes a skeptical response, but that can happen whether it worked or not. Often you'll have an emotional response if you find your purpose—something like, "Oh, that's it!" That emotional response could be fear or anxiety or wanting to believe your purpose is something else. All of that is confirming evidence that you have found your purpose.

If you've really found your blessing, you can look back at your life and see all the ways you've done it over and over and over again. This will only happen if it really worked and it really is your blessing. So having explored these things, you have to decide, "Is this really true? Did it really happen? Is it really my purpose?" If you believe that it's not your purpose, then you must keep looking.

If you decide that it is your purpose, then the next question is, "What do I want to do about it?" That's the sixty-four million dollar question. The answer might be, "Nothing! Forget I asked." If you go on as before, your life will continue pretty much the way it was. Alternatively, you might say, "No, I really want to live a purposeful life, and I want to make changes in my life. Now that I know this is my purpose, I want to say 'no' to things that aren't purposeful, and say 'yes' to things that are purposeful!" Over time this will slowly change your life to make your activities more and more in line with your purpose. It will also bring who you're being more and more in line with your purpose; that will cause you to be happier and more fulfilled, and usually more successful as well. Knowing your purpose by itself does nothing; the changes will come only if you incorporate your purpose into your decision-making.

You will also need to have a relationship with your trusted source. Continue to communicate with it through meditation or prayer or journaling, and have two-way conversations where you ask questions and get answers from the trusted source.

Wright

How do I stay on purpose in my life?

Kelley

One important way is incorporating it into your decision-making. If someone offers you a job, you have to ask yourself the question, "Would taking this job give me more opportunity to live my purpose, or not?" The smart money says that if the new job will allow you to be more purposeful in your life, you will be better at it and therefore more successful.

If the new job seems like a good idea, but it's *not* going to allow you to be more purposeful, it's probably not such a good idea after all. Even though it might look like a smart move, it probably won't work out if it's not purposeful. If you're smart you'll say "no." Even if it looks like it's going to make you a lot of money, it probably won't. Even if it does, you'll probably be unhappy doing it because you will feel unfulfilled. So keep looking for ways to be more purposeful and slowly let go of the things that are not purposeful. This will gradually and steadily change your life.

The other important practice for staying on purpose is to stay in contact with your trusted source. You need to ask it questions and get answers on a regular basis. "Regular" could mean once a week or two; it doesn't need to be every day. But that regular contact really makes a huge difference. If you don't check in with your trusted source regularly, chances are you will lose touch with your purpose and drift back to your old way of being.

Another thing that really helps is to get support from other people who are living a purposeful life. This could be a friend, a coach, an online community or a support group. You need to be around purposeful people because if everyone around you is just talking about money, gossip, and the surface level of reality, you're going to start to feel alone and it will be hard to stay on the path.

Wright

Where can I learn more about life purpose?

Kelley

I have a couple of online communities. One is knowyourpurpose.com; that's for a general audience. If you are interested in finding your life's purpose, you can go there and sign up for a weekly e-zine with tips and information about life purpose. You can also buy CDs, books, and e-books that will teach you specific methods for finding your purpose. If you go to Amazon.com, you'll find thousands of books about purpose, but most of them don't have specific methods for finding it.

For businesspeople there's a different site: www.purposefulleader.com. It teaches about living a purposeful life in business, which leads to more success as a leader and as an organization. There's also a place for coaches, consultants, and therapists: www.purposefulcoach.com is for people who wish to be trained in methods for finding their clients' life purpose.

All of these sites have free e-zines you can subscribe to. If you do, you will be kept up to date on my speaking schedule, upcoming workshops, and other tools for finding your purpose.

Wright

If readers of this book or participants in your workshops were to use these methods to find their purpose—their essence, blessing, and mission, the way you've defined them here—do you think it would make a major positive change in their lives? Would it change their careers? Would it change the way they look at their careers? How does that happen?

Kelley

Once people really get clear on their essence, blessing, and mission, and then turn around and look at their current lives and ask themselves, "How purposefully am I living," it starts to show them the path forward. If you look at the different activities in your life and rate them on how purposeful they are, you might find that you are right on target—that the things you are doing are absolutely purposeful, and that's why you were doing them. You might not have understood your purpose at the time, but now that you know it, you might conclude, "I need to keep doing what I'm doing." If this were the case, you would be able to see *why* you're doing what you're doing and you would be more successful and more fulfilled because you would understand how these activities relate to your purpose.

Sometimes people look at their careers and say, "Okay, this isn't a bad career for me, but how I'm doing it isn't the most purposeful way." If this were the case for you, you might seek a new position within your company or modify your job description to allow you to bring more of your purpose to work. If you were a service professional, like a coach or consultant, you might need to change your marketing material to better reflect your purpose.

On the other hand, sometimes people look at their current job situation and they say, "Wow, this is not purposeful at all! Now I can see why I was so bored and unfulfilled, why I've been chafing at the bit all this time. There's just no opportunity here for me to express my purpose. It's just not going to happen!" This could be the beginning of a process of transitioning to a new career or job that is more purposeful. It takes time—you don't find your purpose one day and walk off your job the next, unless you're independently wealthy. You have to start thinking about what a purposeful position would look like, how you would land it, that sort of thing. You would need to talk to your trusted source about how to find something more purposeful: "What would be a more purposeful career for me? How do I get started? Is there any training I need?" You would start to envision and manifest a more purposeful life—and that transition could take several years.

In the end, though, it is well worth it. I have trouble remembering what it felt like to get up every day and drive to a job that didn't fulfill me. I don't experience what I do as "work"—it's the thing I was born to do, and I can't imagine doing anything else. I wake up every day and I transform people's lives, and I feel deeply grateful that I get to do it. Everyone can have this experience because everyone has a purpose. There is a life of fulfillment and meaning waiting for you. The question is, are you willing to do what it takes to find it and live it?

About the Author

TIM KELLEY has helped many CEOs and top executives find their life's purpose. He has transformed entire organizations by working with their executive teams. His approach brings passion and inspiration throughout the work force and creates bottom line results. Tim's methodology, *Know Your Purpose,* has been featured nationally in magazines and on television.

Tim's clients include Hewlett Packard, American Airlines, ING, Deloitte & Touche, Charles Schwab, and Bayer. He formerly worked as a leader at Oracle, two levels below the CEO. He is coauthor of the best-selling book *Wake Up . . . Live the Life You Love: Living on Purpose.*

Tim has commanded military organizations, including an amphibious assault craft unit, and is a decorated Naval Reserve officer. He holds a bachelor's degree in theoretical mathematics from MIT. Tim lives in Berkeley, California, with his wife, Heather, and son, Ronan.

Tim Kelley
Transcendent Solutions LLC
2024 Eighth Street
Berkeley, CA 94710
415.902.8906
timk@transcendentsolutions.com
www.knowyourpurpose.com

Chapter Two

An interview with...

Stephen R. Covey

David Wright (Wright)

We're talking today with Dr. Stephen R. Covey, cofounder and vice-chairman of Franklin Covey Company, the largest management company and leadership development organization in the world. Dr. Covey is perhaps best known as the author of *The 7 Habits of Highly Effective People* which is ranked as a number one best seller by the *New York Times*, having sold more than fourteen million copies in thirty-eight languages throughout the world. Dr. Covey is an internationally respected leadership authority, family expert, teacher, and organizational consultant. He has made teaching principle-centered living and principle-centered leadership his life's work. Dr. Covey is the recipient of the Thomas More College Medallion for Continuing Service to Humanity and has been awarded four honorary doctorate degrees. Other awards given Dr. Covey include the Sikh's 1989 International Man of Peace award, the 1994 International Entrepreneur of the Year award, *Inc.* magazine's Services Entrepreneur of the Year award, and in 1996 the National Entrepreneur of the Year Lifetime Achievement award for Entrepreneurial leadership. He has also been recognized as one of *Time* magazine's twenty-five most influential Americans and one of Sales and Marketing Management's top twenty-five power brokers. Dr. Covey earned his undergraduate degree from the University of Utah, his MBA from Harvard, and completed his doctorate at Brigham Young University. While at Brigham Young he served as assistant to the President and was also a professor of business management and organizational behavior.

Dr. Covey, welcome to *Blueprint for Success*.

Dr. Stephen Covey (Covey)

Thank you.

Wright

Dr. Covey, most companies make decisions and filter them down through their organization. You, however, state that no company can succeed until individuals within it succeed. Are the goals of the company the result of the combined goals of the individuals?

Covey

Absolutely, because if people aren't on the same page, they're going to be pulling in different directions. To teach this concept, I frequently ask large audiences to close their eyes and point north, and then to keep pointing and open their eyes and they find themselves pointing all over the place. I say to them, "Tomorrow morning if you want a similar experience, ask the first ten people you meet in your organization what the purpose of your organization is and you'll find it's a very similar experience. They'll point all over the place." When people have a different sense of purpose and values, every decision that is made from then on is governed by those. There's no question that this is one of the fundamental causes of misalignment, low trust, interpersonal conflict, interdepartmental rivalry, people operating on personal agendas, and so forth.

Wright

Is that mostly a result of the inability to communicate from the top?

Covey

That's one aspect, but I think it's more fundamental. There's an inability to involve people—an unwillingness. Leaders may communicate what their mission and their strategy is, but that doesn't mean there's any emotional connection to it. Mission statements that are rushed and then announced are soon forgotten. They become nothing more than just a bunch of platitudes on the wall that mean essentially nothing and even create a source of cynicism and a sense of hypocrisy inside the culture of an organization.

Wright

How do companies ensure survival and prosperity in these tumultuous times of technological advances, mergers, downsizing, and change?

Covey

I think that it takes a lot of high trust in a culture that has something that doesn't change—principles—at its core. There are principles that people agree upon that are valued. It gives a sense of stability. Then you have the power to adapt and be flexible when you experience these kinds of disruptive new economic models or technologies that come in and sideswipe you. You don't know how to handle them unless you have something you can depend upon. If people have not agreed to a common set of principles that guide them and a common purpose, then they get their security from the outside and they tend to freeze the structure, systems, and processes inside and they cease becoming adaptable. They don't change with the changing realities of the new marketplace out there and gradually they become obsolete.

Wright

I was interested in one portion of your book *The 7 Habits of Highly Effective People* where you talk about behaviors. How does an individual go about the process of replacing ineffective behaviors with effective ones?

Covey

I think that for most people it usually requires a crisis that humbles them to become aware of their ineffective behaviors. If there's not a crisis the tendency is to perpetuate those behaviors and not change. You don't have to wait until the marketplace creates the crisis for you. Have everyone accountable on a 360 degree basis to everyone else they interact with—with feedback either formal or informal—where they are getting data as to what's happening. They will then start to realize that the consequences of their ineffective behavior require them to be humble enough to look at that behavior and to adopt new, more effective ways of doing things. Sometimes people can be stirred up to this if you just appeal to their conscience—to their inward sense of what is right and wrong. A lot of people sometimes know inwardly they're doing wrong, but the culture doesn't necessarily discourage them from continuing that. They either need feedback from people, or they need feedback from the marketplace, or they need feedback from their conscience. Then they can begin to develop a step-by-step process of replacing old habits with new, better habits.

Wright

It's almost like saying, "Let's make all the mistakes in the laboratory before we put this thing in the air."

Covey

Right; and I also think what is necessary is a paradigm shift, which is analogous to having a correct map, say of a city or of a country. If people have an inaccurate paradigm of life, of other people, and of themselves it really doesn't make much difference what their behavior or habits or attitudes are. What they need is a correct paradigm—a correct map—that describes what's going on. For instance, in the Middle Ages they used to heal people through bloodletting. It wasn't until Samuel Weiss and Pasteur and other empirical scientists discovered the germ theory that they realized for the first time they weren't dealing with the real issue. They realized why women preferred to use midwives who washed rather than doctors who didn't wash. They gradually got a new paradigm. Once you've got a new paradigm then your behavior and your attitude flows directly from it. If you have a bad paradigm or a bad map, let's say of a city, there's no way, no matter what your behavior or your habits or your attitudes are—how positive they are—you'll never be able to find the location you're looking for. This is why I believe that to change paradigms is far more fundamental than to work on attitude and behavior.

Wright

One of your seven habits of highly effective people is to begin with the end in mind. If circumstances change and hardships or miscalculation occurs, how does one view the end with clarity?

Covey

Many people think to begin with the end in mind means that you have some fixed definition of a goal that's accomplished and if changes come about you're not going to adapt to them. Instead, the "end in mind" you begin with is that you are going to create a flexible culture of high trust so that no matter what comes along you are going to do whatever it takes to accommodate that new change or that new reality and maintain a culture of high performance and high trust. You're talking more in terms of values and overall purposes that don't change, rather than specific strategies or programs that will have to change to accommodate the changing realities in the marketplace.

Wright

In this time of mistrust between people, corporations, and nations for that matter, how do we create high levels of trust?

Covey

That's a great question and it's complicated because there are so many elements that go into the creating of a culture of trust. Obviously the most fundamental one is just to have trustworthy people. But that is not sufficient because what if the organization itself is misaligned? For instance, what if you say you value cooperation but you really reward people for internal competition? Then you have a systemic or a structure problem that creates low trust inside the culture even though the people themselves are trustworthy. This is one of the insights of Edward Demming and the work he did. That's why he said that most problems are not personal; they're systemic. They're common caused. That's why you have to work on structure, systems, and processes to make sure that they institutionalize principle-centered values. Otherwise you could have good people with bad systems and you'll get bad results.

When it comes to developing interpersonal trust between people, it is made up of many, many elements such as taking the time to listen to other people, to understand them, and to see what is important to them. What we think is important to another may only be important to us, not to another. It takes empathy. You have to make and keep promises to them. You have to treat them with kindness and courtesy. You have to be completely honest and open. You have to live up to your commitments. You can't betray them behind their back. You can't badmouth them behind their back and sweet-talk them to their face. That will send out vibes of hypocrisy and it will be detected. You have to learn to apologize when you make mistakes, to admit mistakes, and to also get feedback going in every direction as much as possible. It doesn't necessarily require formal forums; it requires trust between people that will be open with each other and give each other feedback.

Wright

My mother told me to do a lot of what you're saying now, but it seems like when I got in business I simply forgot.

Covey

Sometimes we forget, but sometimes culture doesn't nurture it. That's why I say unless you work with the institutionalizing—that means formalizing into structure, systems, and processes the values—you will not have a nurturing culture. You have to constantly work on that. This is one of the big mistakes organizations make. They think trust is simply a function of being honest. That's only one small aspect. It's an important aspect, obviously, but there are so many other elements that go into the creation of a high trust culture.

Wright

"Seek first to understand then to be understood" is another of your seven habits. Do you find that people try to communicate without really understanding what other people want?

Covey

Absolutely. The tendency is to project out of our own autobiography—our own life, our own value system—onto other people, thinking we know what they want. So we don't really listen to them. We pretend to listen, but we really don't listen from within their frame of reference. We listen from within our own frame of reference and we're really preparing our reply rather than seeking to understand. This is a very common thing. In fact very few people have had any training in seriously listening. They're trained in how to read, write, and speak, but not to listen.

Reading, writing, speaking, and listening are the four modes of communication and they represent about two-thirds to three-fourths of our waking hours. About half of that time is spent listening, but it's the one skill people have not been trained in. People have had all this training in the other forms of communication. In a large audience of 1,000 people you wouldn't have more than twenty people who have had more than two weeks of training in listening. Listening is more than a skill or a technique so that you're listening within another frame of reference. It takes tremendous courage to listen because you're at risk when you listen. You don't know what's going to happen; you're vulnerable.

Wright

Sales gurus always tell me that the number one skill in selling is listening.

Covey

Yes—listening from within the customer's frame of reference. That is so true. You can see that it takes some security to do that because you don't know what's going to happen.

Wright

With our *Mission Possible!* book we're trying to encourage people in our audience to be better, to live better, and be more fulfilled by listening to the examples of our guests. Is there anything or anyone in your life that has made a difference for you and helped you to become a better person?

Covey

I think the most influential people in my life have been my parents. I think that what they modeled was not to make comparisons and harbor jealousy or to seek recognition. They were humble people. I remember my mother one time when we were going up in an elevator and the most prominent person in the state was in the elevator. She knew him, but she spent her time talking to the elevator operator. I was just a little kid and I was so awed by this person and I said to my mom, "Why didn't you talk to the important person?" She said, "I was. I had never met him." They were really humble, modest people who were focused on service and other people rather than on themselves. I think they were very inspiring models to me.

Wright

In almost every research paper that anyone I've ever read writes about people who influenced their lives, in the top five people, three of them are teachers. My seventh grade English teacher was the greatest teacher I ever had and influenced me to no end.

Covey

Would it be correct to say that she saw in you probably some qualities of greatness you didn't even see in yourself?

Wright

Absolutely.

Covey

That's been my general experience that the key aspect of a mentor or a teacher is someone who sees in you potential that you don't even see in yourself. They treat you accordingly and eventually you come to see it in yourself. That's my definition of leadership or influence—communicating people's worth and potential so clearly that they are inspired to see it in themselves.

Wright

Most of my teachers treated me as a student, but she treated me with much more respect than that. As a matter of fact, she called me Mr. Wright in the seventh grade. I'd never been addressed by anything but a nickname. I stood a little taller; she just made a tremendous difference. Do you think there are other characteristics that mentors seem to have in common?

Covey

I think they are first of all good examples in their own personal lives. Their personal lives and their family lives are not all messed up—they come from a base of good character. They also are usually very confident and they take the time to do what your teacher did to you—to treat you with uncommon respect and courtesy.

They also, I think, explicitly teach principles rather than practices so that rules don't take the place of human judgment. You gradually come to have faith in your own judgment in making decisions because of the affirmation of such a mentor. Good mentors care about you—you can feel the sincerity of their caring. It's like the expression, "I don't care how much you know until I know how much you care."

Wright

Most people are fascinated with the new television shows about being a survivor. What has been the greatest comeback that you've made from adversity in your career or your life?

Covey

When I was in grade school I experienced a disease in my legs. It caused me to use crutches for a while. I tried to get off them fast and get back. The disease wasn't corrected yet so I went back on crutches for another year. The disease went to the other leg and I went on for another year. It essentially took me out of my favorite thing—athletics—and it took me more into being a student. So that was kind of a life-defining experience which at the time seemed very negative, but has proven to be the basis on which I've focused my life—being more of a learner.

Wright

Principle-centered learning is basically what you do that's different from anybody I've read or listened to.

Covey

The concept is embodied in the far-eastern expression, "Give a man a fish, you feed him for the day; teach him how to fish, you feed him for a lifetime." When you teach principles that are universal and timeless, they don't belong to just any one person's religion or to a particular culture or geography. They seem to be timeless and universal like the ones we've been talking about here: trustworthiness, honesty, caring, service, growth, and development. These are universal principles. If you focus on these things then little by little people become independent of you and then they start to believe in themselves and their own judgment becomes better. You don't need as many rules. You don't need as much bureaucracy and as many controls and you can empower people.

The problem in most business operations today—and not just business but non-business—is that they're using the industrial model in an information age. Arnold Toynbee, the great historian, said, "You can pretty well summarize all of history in four words: nothing fails like success." The industrial model was based on the asset of the machine. The information model is based on the asset of the person—the knowledge worker. It's an altogether different model. But the machine model was the main asset of the twentieth century. It enabled productivity to increase fifty times. The new asset is intellectual and social capital—the qualities of people and the quality of the relationship they have with each other. Like Toynbee said, "Nothing fails like success." The industrial model does not work in an information age. It requires a focus on the new wealth, not capital and material things.

A good illustration that demonstrates how much we were into the industrial model, and still are, is to notice where people are on the balance sheet. They're not found there. Machines are found there. Machines become investments. People are on the profit and loss statement and people are expenses. Think of that—if that isn't bloodletting.

Wright

It sure is.

When you consider the choices you've made down through the years, has faith played an important role in your life?

Covey

It has played an extremely important role. I believe deeply that we should put principles at the center of our lives, but I believe that God is the source of those principles. I did not invent them. I get credit sometimes for some of the Seven Habits material and some of the other things I've done, but it's really all based on principles that have been given by God to all of His children from the beginning of time. You'll find that you can teach these same principles from the sacred texts and the wisdom literature of almost any tradition. I think the ultimate source of that is God and that is one thing you can absolutely depend upon—in God we trust.

Wright

If you could have a platform and tell our audience something you feel would help them or encourage them, what would you say?

Covey

I think I would say to put God at the center of your life and then prioritize your family. No one on their deathbed ever wished they spent more time at the office.

Wright

That's right. We have come down to the end of our program and I know you're a busy person, but I could talk with you all day Dr. Covey.

Covey

It's good to talk with you as well and to be a part of this program. It looks like an excellent one that you've got going on here.

Wright

Thank you.

We have been talking today with Dr. Stephen R. Covey, co-founder and vice-chairman of Franklin Covey Company. He's also the author of *The 7 Habits of Highly Effective People,* which has been ranked as a number one bestseller by the *New York Times*, selling more than fourteen million copies in thirty-eight languages.

Dr. Covey, thank you so much for being with us today.

Covey

Thank you for the honor of participating.

About The Author

STEPHEN R. COVEY was recognized in 1996 as one of *Time* magazine's twenty-five most influential Americans and one of Sales and Marketing Management's top twenty-five power brokers. Dr. Covey is the author of several acclaimed books, including the international bestseller, *The 7 Habits of Highly Effective People*. It has sold more than fifteen million copies in thirty-eight languages throughout the world. Other bestsellers authored by Dr. Covey include *First Things First, Principle-Centered Leadership* (with sales exceeding one million), and *The 7 Habits of Highly Effective Families.*

Dr. Covey's newest book, *The 8th Habit: From Effectiveness to Greatness,* which was released in November 2004, rose to the top of several bestseller lists, including *New York Times, Wall Street Journal, USA Today, Money, Business Week,* and Amazon.com and Barnes & Noble. *The 8th Habit . . .* has sold more than 360,000 copies.

Dr. Covey earned his undergraduate degree from the University of Utah, his MBA from Harvard, and completed his doctorate at Brigham Young University. While at Brigham Young University, he served as assistant to the President and was also a professor of business management and organizational behavior. He received the National Fatherhood Award in 2003, which, as the father of nine and grandfather of forty-four, he says is the most meaningful award he has ever received.

Dr. Covey currently serves on the board of directors for the Points of Light Foundation. Based in Washington, D.C., the Foundation, through its partnership with the Volunteer Center National Network, engages and mobilizes millions of volunteers from all walks of life—businesses, nonprofits, faith-based organizations, low-income communities, families, youth, and older adults—to help solve serious social problems in thousands of communities.

Dr. Stephen R. Covey
www.stephencovey.com

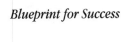
Blueprint for Success

Chapter Three

An interview with...

Bill Treasurer &
Ahli Moore

David Wright (Wright)

Today we are talking with Bill Treasurer and Ahli Moore. Giant Leap Consulting is a courage-building company whose mission is to help people and organizations be more courageous.

GLC's founder and Chief Encouragement Officer, Bill Treasurer, believes that courage is the first business virtue because it makes all the other virtues possible. Leadership, innovation, and entrepreneurship all require large doses of courage."

GLC's President and COO, Ahli Moore, is living proof of GLC's courage credo, leaving a lucrative corporate job with a highly respected international management consulting firm to support GLC's mission of courageous living. GLC has four primary service offerings: Courageous Future (Strategic Planning), Courageous Leadership (Leadership Development), Courageous Teaming (Teambuilding), and Courageous Development (Customized Training).

Bill and Ahli, welcome to *Blueprint for Success!*

Bill Treasurer (Treasurer)

We're pleased to be part of this book project.

Wright

What prompted your interest in "courage"?

Treasurer

I had a debilitating fear of heights when I was young, and over time I was able to work through that fear with the help of a patient coach. Ultimately, I learned how to dominate my fear so much that I eventually I became a world-class high diver. I performed over 1,500 dives from heights that scaled to over 100 feet (the equivalent of a ten-story building).

So I learned firsthand the benefits of finding and using my courage. I thought, wouldn't it be great to take the lessons I learned on my journey to overcome my fear of heights and use them to help people and organizations overcome whatever fears and anxieties—their "high dives"—they might be facing. Having taken a bunch of giant leaps myself, my company now helps others take giant leaps as well.

Wright

You described Giant Leap Consulting as a "courage-building company." What does that mean?

Treasurer

The mission of Giant Leap Consulting is to help people and organizations be more courageous. We do that in four ways:

1. We work with companies to help them develop *bold vision*—vision that helps them inspire people to want to follow them. Through our **Courageous Future** service line we help companies create bold strategies.

2. New strategies often require new leadership behaviors. We develop courage in leaders so they can take *direct action* toward the achievement of the strategies. GLC has created a broad portfolio of leadership workshops, and in most cases they are co-facilitated with leaders from our client companies. We call this service line **Courageous Leadership**.

3. Leaders execute strategies through teams. So we work with teams to build *sustained momentum* toward the attainment of the strategic goals. **Courageous Teaming**, our third service line, involves learning how to team with one another in a more honest, noble, and courageous way.

4. Finally, we help companies continuously *elevate performance* by conducting skill-building workshops that enable workers to stretch both their skills and their comfort zones. This service line is called **Courageous Development**.

Our four courage-building services aim at creating *bold visions,* leaders who take *direct action,* teams that execute with *sustained momentum,* and a workforce that continuously *elevates performance* of the company and themselves.

Ahli Moore (Moore)

Those are the four primary service offerings that GLC provides. However, something that differentiates us from many other companies is that we don't have a prescriptive list of answers for your personal courage issues or predetermined steps for your specific courage needs. What we do is customize programs around what the individual in your organization requires. We accomplish that by conducting thorough, up-front stakeholder interviews with all of the key players in the organization and analyzing the interactions among the people. Only then can we customize the four service offerings that Bill described into specific steps and behaviors that inspire changes resulting in courageous decision-making in their everyday activities.

Wright

What are some of the examples of the courage-building work you've done with clients?

Treasurer

One of our clients is Aldridge Electric Company, a large specialty electrical contractor in Chicago. These are the folks who put in all the runway lights at O'Hare Airport. They're the same folks who keep the lights on at Soldier Field. It's quite a big electrical construction company, and Giant Leap facilitates their strategic planning process to help Aldridge develop bold, competition-eclipsing strategies.

One of their recent big decisions was to enter into the power market, specifically in the emerging area of wind farms. A lot of emphasis is being placed on alternative energy sources these days. Wind farms generate electricity, and Aldridge is in the electricity business, so there was a strategic complement.

With Aldridge's new strategic direction came a new set of leadership marching orders, so we worked with Aldridge's leadership team to develop a comprehensive leadership development curriculum consisting of ten workshops customized around the needs of the company. The program takes ten months to complete and is cascading to all of Aldridge's leaders throughout the company. Aldridge's "high potential" leaders are now developing the necessary capabilities to lead the company into new markets and into the future.

The key is that in addition to helping Aldridge develop sound business strategies that are bold and courageous, we are also working with their leaders to make sure that they are being courageous enough to lead the people into the future that they are trying to create.

Moore

We were recently involved in a very unique engagement that was a combination of both Courageous Future and Courageous Leadership. Accenture, a global leader in management consulting, and Cayuse Technologies, a new information technology company owned by the Confederated Tribes of the Umatilla Indian Reservation (CTUIR), entered into a five-year agreement to provide technology services to governmental and commercial clients. Approximately 50 percent of the company's estimated 250 employees will come from the Umatilla tribe, another 10 percent will be comprised of Indians from other tribes, and the remaining 40 percent will be non-Indian. This first-of-its-kind venture is at once groundbreaking, courageous, and opportunistic, providing sustainable economic development for the Umatilla people while allowing Accenture to provide competitive rates for business process outsourcing services delivered "on shore."

Although the idea was both noble and exciting, it did not come without challenges, most prominent of which was cultural incompatibility. What makes a person successful at Accenture is quite different from what makes a person successful as part of the Native American Indian community. GLC was tasked with helping to build a culture that is distinctly Indian in its identity, but also includes Accenture's disciplined approach to management and work.

Giant Leap developed a workshop to leverage and integrate the best cultural attributes of both Accenture and the CTUIR by:

1. Working directly with Cayuse Technology's employees to identify the cultural values and attributes of their heritage to bring forward into the new company—*defining who we are.*
2. Leading the employees in developing a robust set of core values to strengthen the organization and position it for future success—*owning the core values.*
3. Providing a forum to both explain the journey ahead and build the cultural roadmap to get there—*inspiring a shared vision of the future.*
4. Gaining commitment from employees on the individual behaviors that will support the core values—*living the core values.*

Moore

Another example is courageous team building, and it's actually a combination of all four GLC offerings. We've developed a program called the NOC MBA, where MBA stands for Management By Adventure. In this program we take our clients offsite to the Nantahala Outdoor Center in North Carolina for a combination of inside the classroom *lecturettes* and outside the classroom activities, including a high ropes course and whitewater rafting. The activities are designed to challenge the participants physically, analytically, and really test their boundaries for personal courage and their courage as a team. Through these activities participants get an opportunity to: (1) catch themselves being themselves, (2) bond together as a team, and (3) to go to (discussion) places they typically wouldn't discuss while they're in the workplace. Through the outdoor activities and the inside the classroom activities participants get the opportunity to really express themselves and understand more about what motivates them individually and gives them the courage to test their own boundaries.

Wright

How do you help organizations build courage?

Treasurer

The first thing we do is get very close to the objectives of the organization and what they are trying to achieve. Based on that, we design the courage-building approaches that are most appropriate given their goals.

Many organizations have touchy, "off limit" subjects that avoiding only worsens. Sometimes we'll hear people say, "Whatever you do, don't go there." Often the "theres" are the things holding a company back because they are the truest sign of low trust levels among people. What we do is work with the organization to create enough trust within the system so that they can actually *go there*.

The techniques we use to help a company "go there" vary based on the needs of a company. But one example is what we call a "pink elephant session." Pink elephants are those politically delicate subjects that everybody sees in the middle of the room, but nobody wants to address. To address the pink elephants, we first lay down a set of ground rules and get everyone's commitment to abide by them. Then we conduct a very structured conversation whereby each individual is allowed to state his or her perception of the *elephant* and its causes—without interruption (which is key). It's actually quite a demanding process, particularly on the facilitator directing the conversation.

Pink elephant sessions are just one of the techniques we use, and there are a host of others.

Moore

Like any other consulting firm we have a list of frameworks and theories that we use to structure our thoughts and suggestions. But to Bill's point, by getting close to the actual objective we allow the participants to operationalize their own vision. It's not enough to just say, "As a company we need to communicate better." What we want them to do is get very specific and talk about the actions and behaviors that led them to where they are now so we can help them to make a courageous leap to where they want to be in the future. Through things like the pink elephant sessions, we actually outline the behaviors that may be detrimental to their current success, and start to build the behaviors they'll be measured by as they go forward!

Wright

Why do you think there's so much fear in the workplace these days?

Treasurer

There are a number of reasons. At a macro level is globalization. In general, globalization has been good for many businesses, but it has also made markets very sensitive to uncontrollable factors happening in other parts of the world. Things that happen in China or in Asia or in South America can ripple to the United States in an instant creating a very volatile business environment. This volatility is exacerbated by the Internet because small up-starts can be Little David's taking on Big Goliaths, doing serious damage in the process. Combine these factors with the very real possibilities of terrorism, and it serves to inject fear throughout all the arteries of commerce.

One of our clients is a large agricultural pharmaceutical company, and after 9/11, for the very first time, they started talking about the possibility of agro-terrorism. This company is actually very worried about some types of biological agents being put into the food system. When you are working in that kind of environment it presents a new kind of fear that is imbued into the workplace, and that fear starts to permeate the system, ultimately directing people's behaviors.

Despite the great management philosophies of the twenty-first century about how to treat people at work, when leaders are under a tremendous amount of stress and competitive pressure, they start to adopt outdated but easily applied behavior like intimidation or bullying. You'd think that given everyone's access to progressive management theories, such practices would be long gone by now. What we find, unfortunately, is that the stressors of the modern age have actually increased abusive leadership behavior and by default, the permeation of fear in the workplace.

These are very, very fearful times in the workplace. We consider Giant Leap's mission of helping people and organizations be more courageous to be a near spiritual calling. The bottom line is that we're in the business of driving out fear from the workplace. Driving out fear, coincidently, is the ultimate goal of nearly every major religion, and we approach our mission with the same zeal.

We believe that people perform better out of competence, courage, and conviction than fear. Fear lowers standards, quality, and profits. Fear produces nearly everything that's bad at work, such as bullying, micromanagement, brownnosing, ass-covering, safe strategies, inequitable compensation practices, burned-out employees, low morale, and crappy attitudes.

Moore

I'll also add that many people talk about the current lack of loyalty in the workplace. In reality it goes both ways with employers not being loyal to employees, and employees not being loyal to employers. I would actually challenge that just a bit to say that there's a *perceived* lack of loyalty. But what's probably more accurate is that there is a change in today's business models and work dynamics in which all jobs aren't designed for long-term tenure the way they used to be. And all employees don't desire to be in certain positions for many years the way they used to be. But because of that perceived "lack of loyalty" and our inability to adjust to the different paradigm shifts in the business model, often we are not prepared to face the employee whose intention is to only be here for five years. We're still trying to use the same set of rules and parameters that we used years ago when we expected an employee to be there for a long time. It goes the same way for the employee's relationship with a set of rules that he or she may be using with the employer. I think the lack of loyalty *or the perceived lack of loyalty* infuses fear into the workplace a bit.

To add to another one of Bill's points, the instant success of companies with the advent of the Internet compels larger incumbents to feel like they must take shortcuts out of fear that they are falling behind the curve. Sometimes these reactive shortcuts are not balanced with courageous risk-taking and lead to disastrous results.

Wright

Who are some business people that you consider to be courageous?

Treasurer

Fortunately, Giant Leap Consulting seems to attract clients who are more interested in being courageous than fearful. I've already mentioned one example with the Aldridge Electric Company. Another example is Sara Blakely, the founder of Spanx, a women's apparel company. Sara invented (and patented) a seamless girdle-like undergarment. Women love the fact that Spanx products don't show those lumpy seams that come through when wearing products from other apparel makers. The bottom line is that Spanx's products make woman more attractive.

What makes Sara courageous is that she started Spanx literally out of her basement. When you meet Sara you recognize her as a person who is willing to confront her fears. She had a fear of speaking in public, for example, that caused her to become a stand-up comedian. Later on she was a contestant on Richard Branson's television show, *The Rebel Billionaire,* and came in second place after a grueling ten-week process. Richard Branson ended up giving her $750,000 and asking her to lead a new foundation dedicated to creating opportunities for women.

Sara is a very courageous woman and she's doing great things for women and business in general. She's one of our favorite clients; we've worked with her company for the past three years and we're pleased to do so. I'm also pleased to tell you that Sara wrote the forward to my forthcoming book, *Courage Goes to Work*.

Moore

And I'd add that we see many people like Sara Blakely and we see the nationally and world-renowned figures, and we can say that these are people who show a lot of courage. But there are also people who are not in positions of authority, they're not widely known, but they display courage in their everyday actions, whether at work or in their personal lives.

A good example is a very junior member of another client team with whom we do a lot of business. She recently told me of an example when she called a halt to an important meeting because there were some numbers that had been miscalculated. And by doing so she was putting the account and the work they were doing for that client in jeopardy. But her courageous action was to say, "These numbers are incorrect; we've miscalculated the results. And because of this, whether we need to put a halt to this project or whether we need to redo the work, we need to do what's right. We may lose face on this, we may lose some of our reputation, or we may gain reputation by saying we are an honest and trustworthy company." Unlike what I've seen other people do (try to justify, hide, or cover up the numbers), she raised her hand

and said they needed to take another look at this. It actually turned out for the better.

That's an example of someone who isn't going to be on television, isn't going to be on the front page of *Business Week,* but her personal, courageous act (it's part of a framework that we talk about—the courage to tell) was an example of a businessperson showing a lot of courage that most will never read about.

Wright

So what can the average worker do to be a little bit more courageous at work?

Treasurer

One thing they can do is make what I call a "Life-Orienting Decision"— an LOD. Before you can pursue courageous endeavors you have to be resolved to living a life of courage. And that means making a fundamental decision—a commitment—to engaging with fear. Once you make an LOD you begin to face challenging or fear-inspiring situations with more courage. Giant Leap's motto is really an LOD: Be Courageous!

Moore

It's never okay to be a malcontent. And what I mean by that is it's okay to disagree with someone's philosophy or approach to something. What isn't okay is to pretend to agree on the surface and then sit back and shoot arrows at the idea (i.e., six months down the road say that you never agreed with the approach). If you disagree with something, then the courageous thing to do is to say, "I agree on some of your points, but I disagree on others, so let's discuss where we agree and where we differ, and make a mutual decision on this." So it's okay to disagree as long as you *go there* with the conversation to understand what the desired outcome should be.

GLC has developed a framework called the Courage to Try, Trust, and Tell. These concepts offer a way that you can infuse courage into your work life and into your personal life.

Treasurer

TRY Courage is the courage of action. This is the type of courage we associate with "stepping up to the plate" or demonstrating leadership. *TRY Courage* is found in pioneering events—doing things you've never done before. When Aldridge Electric decided to enter the power market, for example, this was *TRY Courage.*

TRUST Courage is the courage of *in*action, or letting go. A good example of the courage to trust is delegation. A lot of middle management people with control issues see their employees doing something and it's not being done the way that they would do it themselves. They feel that if the employee screws up it's going to be a reflection on them as managers, and so they take the task back, effectively undermining the employee who was given the task in the first place. So *TRUST Courage* involves helping managers get to the level of skill where they can actually "let go" and not feel that they have to hover around the person for it to get done. It does involve courage because it means putting yourself at risk when somebody else does something that might become a reflection on you.

The third type of courage is *TELL Courage*—the courage of asserting our true voice. People will say that honesty is the most important value, but then they will hold back their honesty because letting people know what they "really think" could get them in trouble. It's amazing how many client problems are caused by people withholding or hiding from the truth. *TELL Courage* involves creating an environment where people can have healthy, sober, and adult conversations about difficult issues.

Wright

According to Giant Leap Consulting there's a difference between Risk Management and what you call Risk Leadership. Will you explain the difference?

Treasurer

Many leaders in organizations overly preoccupy themselves with Risk Management—the mitigation, control, and minimizing of risk. Giant Leap Consulting says great, keep your company safe. At the same time, if you want to grow and be innovative, you are going to have to *take* risks too. And when you want to take risks, things shift from Risk Management to Risk *Leadership*.

As a former high diver, I tell leaders that preparation will help them lower their high dive only so much. At some point they're still going to have to jump off that high dive ladder if they want to be successful! Giant Leap helps companies become risk leaders, not risk managers.

Moore

And Bill's actually being somewhat humble; he's written another book titled, *Right Risk*. In it he discusses defining your motivations for taking the risks that you take. So when we talk about Risk *Leadership* at Giant Leap, it's exactly what Bill just said—if you want your company to grow, then there are a certain number of risks you have to take. If you're happy with where you are and you want to always be in the same position, then never take a risk. Even if you're experiencing success, if you want to always be impacted by other worldly and industry events and not be able to address them, then never take a risk. But if you want to stay in front of the changes in both business and society, then you're going to have to take some risks somewhere.

Those calculated risks all depend on your personal and your organization's appetite for risk and risk behavior. Books like *Right Risk* and companies like Giant Leap Consulting are here to help people understand risk and that "risk" is not a bad four-letter word. Risk is something that can be healthy and help your organization grow.

Wright

I've heard that your company believes that everyone wants to make a difference. If that's true why do you think it's difficult for people to be more courageous in their daily decision-making?

Treasurer

Well, think about it—ever since you were a little kid you've been taught things like "don't play with matches," "don't cross the street without looking both ways," "don't get too close to the edge." From an early age we've been taught all the "don'ts." It makes sense—our parents wanted to keep us safe. However, when we grow up and allow our behaviors to be dictated by the outdated tapes of our parents, we develop a "play it safe at all costs" mentality, which is dangerous for business.

I think that people who only "play it safe" ultimately live a joyless life. I think the better path is to extend yourself and learn to live in your Courage Zone. I believe this so deeply that I've just finished writing a new book titled *Courage Goes to Work*. It helps people access their Courage Zones.

I have a little saying on the wall in my Asheville office. It says, "And the day came when the risks of remaining tight in a bulb was more dangerous than the risk it took to blossom."

Giant Leap Consulting is in the blossom business, because we like to help people to find the courage that's inside them and let it out!

Wright

How does courage play a role in a highly effective teaming?

Moore

I think that teams are extensions of the individuals who are within that team, and the dynamics of the team are often constrained by our individual ability to understand ourselves, let alone each other. When most companies talk about team dynamics they start focusing on, "What can I do to impact others?" Giant Leap's philosophy is before you can impact the rest of the team you have to say, "What can I do to impact myself?" Take an introspective look at your behaviors and ask yourself if you're making the right decisions: "Am I taking the courageous steps and making the courageous decisions?" You must do that first before you can even start to broach the subject of *team* success.

What role does courage play in highly effective teams? I think that the number one thing that courage does is it allows the individual team members to understand more about themselves, and understanding "why" they make the decisions they make. Understanding where they are in the *courage continuum* first, and then looking at the team is probably the approach I would take.

Treasurer

The only thing I would add is that a lot of teams that don't work well suffer from blame—people point fingers at one another for not getting things done, and a lot of times they don't even do it verbally. They blame people by holding resentment against them or maybe they'll tell one other person on the team so it becomes a gossip kind of situation. We find that one of the most difficult things to do on a team is to confront one another in an adult-like and courageous way. That means having courageous conversations. So some of Giant Leap's work involves helping team members interact with one another in a more courageous and candid way (by using *TELL Courage*).

Wright

What role does courage play in being a successful leader?

Treasurer

First of all, leadership involves bold vision. It's not enough to have a safe and lukewarm vision that doesn't inspire people. The most inspiring visions are ones that make us simultaneously excited and afraid. So the first thing that leaders have to do is come up with a vision that is inspiring and courageous. In fact, for the vision to be most inspiring, it should require the courage of the entire workforce as well.

Second, leaders have to be willing to do pioneering things, even if those things are upsetting in the short-run. An example is one of our clients, whose customers are large automotive companies. For years they provided analytical data and industry information to their clients for free as an amenity to their services. Then they realized that the data they were providing was of a higher quality than even Wall Street provided. In fact, many Wall Street analysts were drawing their conclusions from this company's data. Plus, other companies were charging for lesser quality data. All this caused our client to conclude, "We really need to start charging for the data that we're providing."

Imagine charging customers for something you used to provide for free. This was a bold move with upside and downside potential. On the upside, it gave our client a new revenue stream, and frankly one that they deserved. The downside was that in the short-run their customers were going to complain about paying for something they previously got for free.

That's an example of a visionary leader who said, "Business is a mutual exchange of value. When we add value to our customers, we should be justly rewarded for doing so."

Moore

I'd also add that through most organizations, regardless of your level, you take your behavioral queues from your leader. If you are an analyst, you may take it from the manager above you. If you're a manager, you may take your behavioral queues from the director above you. So it's infusing that courage at each step of the organization; it's not just enough to say that we have a courageous leader—we must continually build courageous leaders throughout the entire organization. Each person's ability to assess his or her own capabilities in what we call a sober manner, and understand what makes that person tick is tantamount to success in any organization.

Courage plays a big part in not only the leader at the top, but throughout the organization at every level.

Wright

Finally, what do both of you think is the most important thing that you'd like the readers of this book to know about courage?

Treasurer

The great philosophers have said that courage is the first virtue because it makes all the other virtues possible. We at Giant Leap Consulting have come to find that it's also the first business virtue. In fact we think that courage is just as important, if not more important, than attributes like leadership, entrepreneurialism, and innovation. Leadership requires bold vision, and it may mean that people will not follow that vision or some will reject that vision, therefore it requires courage. Innovation requires coming up with groundbreaking, but tradition-defined ideas, therefore it takes courage. Entrepreneurialism requires knocking on doors in the face of rejection therefore it takes courage. If that's the case, then this means that if you take courage out of the equation, leadership and entrepreneurialism and innovation don't even exist! So therefore we think that courage is the most important of all business virtues.

What I'd like to leave readers with is that they should not only be courageous in their lives but be courageous in their work lives as well.

Moore

And I might add that courage is not something that has to be relegated to military people or police officers or firemen—while they are certainly examples of courage. Each one of us is an example of courage in what we decide to do with our own lives each day. Exploring the concepts of courage and embracing the ideas of courage are things we should do continuously. Doing this is not a one-time thing—it's something that's personal and we need to do these things weekly, monthly, and annually.

You need to sit down and really assess where you are. Are you doing the things that give you personal fulfillment and joy? Are you doing the things that make the world better? Are you doing the things that make your company better? And if the answer is "no" to any one of those things, then perhaps you should examine your own personal courage and conviction.

Wright

This has been a great conversation, and I really appreciate both of you taking the time to answer these questions!

About the Authors

BILL TREASURER is founder and Chief Encouragement Officer of Giant Leap Consulting. He is the author of *Right Risk* (Berrett-Koehler, 2003), and chief editor and co-author of *Positively M.A.D.* (Berrett-Koehler, 2005). Bill has worked with over seventy-five prominent clients and his insights have been featured in over one hundred national magazines and newspapers. His newest book, *Courage Goes to Work*, is scheduled to be released in 2008. Treasurer was the captain of the U.S. High Diving Team, and performed over 1,500 high dives from heights that scaled to over one hundred feet. Bill and his family live in Asheville, North Carolina.

AHLI MOORE is the President and COO of Giant Leap Consulting. He is a Human Performance expert with over fifteen years of organizational development experience. Since 1993, Ahli has worked with senior executives, training organizations, and human resource departments to increase employee performance and organization efficiency across a multitude of industries. He has consulted for several Fortune 500 companies to develop customized performance management programs.

Among others, marquee clients benefiting from GLC's courage-building services include: Accenture, Merial, Mercedes, the U.S. Veterans Administration, The Home Depot, Spanx, Aldridge Electric Company, Equity Office Properties, Manheim, Inc., and the Drug Enforcement Administration.

Bill Treasurer and Ahli Moore

Giant Leap Consulting
2 Lynnwood Road
Asheville NC 28804

3936 Glen Park Drive
Lithonia, GA 30038
Phone: 800.867.7239
E-mail: info@giantleapconsulting.com
www.giantleapconsulting.com

Chapter Four

Steve Douglas

David Wright (Wright)

Today we're talking with Steve Douglas. Steve brings more than thirty years of professional sales experience that involves three different industries. His clients have included professional athletes, universities, major corporations, manufacturers, and entrepreneurs alike. Steve has spoken to such groups as State Farm Insurance Companies, The Insurance and Financial Advisors Association for the State of Alaska, The National Association of Property Managers, and many athletic sports events for The University of Florida.

Steve I appreciate your participation in *Blueprint for Success;* it's a great book.

What is the message that you want people to hear so they can learn from your success?

Steve Douglas (Douglas)

First, I would like to thank you very much and let you know how honored I am that Insight Publishing has invited me to participate in this meaningful project with Dr. Covey and Dr. Blanchard. For many years I've been a huge fan of both and many of their insightful books are in my personal library.

It is absolutely foundational and paramount to live daily with one's true, unique, and authentic purpose. I discovered my life's purpose early one winter's morning several years ago while vacationing in Canada and it has made all the difference in the world.

There are a couple of famous quotes that I would like to share with our readers:

- "Firmness of purpose is one of the most necessary sinews of character and one of the best instruments of success. Without it, genius wastes its efforts in a maze of inconsistencies."
  —Lord Chesterfield

- "The man without a purpose is like a ship without a rudder— a waif, a nothing, a no man. Have a purpose in life and having it, throw such strength of mind into your work as God has given you."
—Thomas Carlyle

Wright

Do our readers have the same opportunity to discover their purpose with the individual process that you developed and used?

Douglas

Absolutely, that is why I am so excited to share this experience because it will create a life changing moment in one's life as it has in mine. You will find that you no longer just live but now begin to *really* live.

Wright

How does one go about uncovering one's true, unique, and authentic purpose?

Douglas

By voice, as in inner voice. In Dr. Stephen Covey's bestseller *The Eighth Habit,* he states that when you find your voice and inspire others to find their voice you will now create an opportunity to live a life of greatness. He refers to conscience as that still, small voice within—your calling, your soul's code. The reason that so many people don't have a clue as to how to identify their purpose is due to the fact that life is filled with so much change, confusion, noise, and endless chatter. What I have found is that you must create for yourself a very quiet, reflective, and heartfelt state. You need to become very intentional in your search for purpose.

What I have found to be true is that when you put out your *emotional welcome mat* to voice, your voice will graciously appear from your reverent invitation. Your voice will now be your guide to your purpose. What you will discover, though, is that your voice will not communicate with you through sound or hearing. It will emotionally connect with the inner core of your being by feelings and emotions, things like goose bumps and butterflies.

For me, *finding one's purpose is like coming home for the first and last time*. It feels like coming home for the first time because it feels so different and so surreal than what you have ever experienced. It feels like coming home for the last time in that it feels so magnificent and so spectacular that you will not venture far from your newfound home of unparalleled significance, indescribable joy, and unshakeable peace.

Wright

Is it important to balance success in your life?

Douglas

Absolutely, I love the Latin word *pondera,* which means balance. Pondera is a balance of success, not just in one's career, but also in one's relationships and in one's personal and spiritual life. If you want total confirmation that your purpose is authentic, then it should interconnect with all four of these areas.

For me, one of the greatest emotional states to be in, in terms of mature and anchored balance, is when one feels truly worthy of life's many blessings, but in equal measure, be and remain ever grateful for those many blessings.

I'm involved with a national study group that meets once a year for a week to focus on the expansion of our human growth and potential. One of our members who has a successful business in Columbus, Ohio, gave me an Ohio State buckeye. I carry this buckeye with me wherever I go. The only time it is not with me is when I'm either sleeping or in the shower. I make reference to it as my "grateful eye." It is a constant reminder about the importance of gratitude. My heart is always in a grateful state. I found that by choosing to trust an attitude of gratitude I will be left with nothing but the good stuff and I will be able to leave all the collective junk of life right where it belongs—in the junk yard and not in me.

Wright

What do you think are the biggest obstacles people face in trying to be successful?

Douglas

Without a doubt, it is a lack of one's purpose. In a recent national survey conducted in the United States among eighty-five-year-old and older males and females, they were asked that if they could go back and relive their lives, what were some of the things they would do differently. There were three main responses from this insightful group:

- They would take greater risks in their life.
- They would reflect more.
- They would be more involved with something much bigger than themselves.

If you and I and our readers are fortunate enough to live to eighty-five years or older and we have lived with purpose, then these three areas of regret would not be a concern for any of us. What I have discovered in observing others living with purpose is that you will naturally become a much greater risk-taker.

I am not saying that one will now visit Las Vegas frequently and take up parachuting, but what I am saying is that one starts breaking out of their safe, cushy, and comfortable personal comfort zone.

The irony of this is that others will perceive you as taking many risks. Your viewpoint, however, is that you are not really taking a risk at all, but more of a natural free flowing path of human expansion and personal contribution to mankind. Because one makes far greater contribution in serving others than in serving oneself, you will have many wonderful and beautiful memories and moments to reflect on when you find purpose. When you think about it, the whole foundation and essence of purpose is all about creating a life that becomes much larger than oneself.

Wright

Would you mind sharing with our readers your purpose?

Douglas

Not at all—my purpose is to serve and to inspire in making a positive and profound difference in the lives of others.

Wright

Will you share a personal life experience that has created a positive and profound difference in your life?

Douglas

I had the good fortune to view a short five- to six-minute film many years ago. Even though this is one of the shortest films I have ever seen, it had a powerful and profound message and has made a huge impact and difference in my life.

The film starts out with a beautiful morning setting at the beach. The sun is just coming up and you can hear the sound of the seagulls and the waves gently rolling on the beach. In a minute or so you notice there are two men on the beach in opposite direction of each other and they are slowly walking toward one another. In another minute or so you notice that one of the two men is occasionally bending over and it appears as if he's tossing something back into the water. The other man you observe appears to be walking around and stepping over something in his path. Now it dawns on you that what is happening—there are hundreds upon hundreds of little fish washing up on the shore and many of them are left helpless on the sand and will soon meet their impending fate. In another minute or so the two men are approaching each other and you hear a conversation that goes something like this:

"Good morning."

"Good morning to you sir; it sure is a beautiful morning."

"It sure is."

"Sir, I don't mean to sound funny but I've noticed that every so often you are bending over and tossing some fish back to sea. I am sure you, like me, can see there are hundreds of fish dying all around us. I was curious as to what kind of a difference your actions could possibly make?"

The other man casually bent over and picked up a fish and gently pitched it into the water. After watching the fish swim back to sea, he turned, smiled, and said softly but firmly, "It makes a difference to *that* one."

The moral of this story is that you and I might want to help make a difference for everyone in this hurting world but unfortunately that isn't going to happen. What we can do is choose to make a difference for someone. Even if that someone is for only one, then it is in that one, which will make all the difference in the world.

Wright

That is a moving story, Steve. Would you share with us how you motivate others in hopes of making a difference in their lives?

Douglas

I will never ever want to motivate anyone but I am ever grateful when I experience the blessing of inspiring another. The very first time I wrote my purpose on paper I had no idea how compelling and noteworthy it was that my voice chose the word *"inspire"* for me and not *"motivate."*

Wright

What makes your perspective about these two words so unique?

Douglas

After finding my purpose I became very curious and intrigued by how most people use these two words almost interchangeably. After further study, what I discovered was not only enlightening but also shocking to say the least. When people find their purpose and give it freely to the needs of the world, many times they are not even aware that they are now in the process of detaching and disconnecting from personal motivation. They now start connecting, embracing, and taking ownership with inspiration. This transformation is so monumental and life changing that I've coined a phrase to honor the moment when it takes root in one's life:

*"Choose to have your perspiration, (*your life's work), *come from inspiration and not motivation, so that you may now put an end to a life of quiet desperation."*

Henry David Thoreau had one of the most profound and yet sad observations about mankind when he said in his famous quote, "Most men lead lives of quiet desperation."

The quiet translates to *no voice* or *no purpose.* Desperation symbolizes emptiness and restlessness within because there is a deep and disturbing hunger for a life that has far more meaning and significance. The reason people use the words "motivation" and "inspiration" interchangeably is the fact that their one similarity causes confusion and creates false perception. Their one similarity is that they both attain results. Other than the result similarity, they are as opposite as darkness and light. The radical difference is in the *way* the results are attained. This *way* is what I make reference to as one's *emotional dance* with others and their *emotional dance* with life itself. You see, motivation is all about what you do *to* others and inspiration is all about what you do *for* others; and, it's in this difference that will make all the difference in the world. If motivation is the sound to your emotional dance, then you will have a far greater likelihood of not just stepping on, bruising, and wounding the toes of those you are emotionally dancing with, but also wounding their heart, mind, and spirit.

With this I say, invite inspiration to be the composer and conductor for the lyrics, melody, and music to your emotional dance. Using inspiration as the beat of your emotional dance, you will find it far more elegant, natural, and free flowing.

Wright

Would you clarify for me why the *way* that results are attained is so dramatically different?

Douglas

According to the *Random House Dictionary,* inspiration is described in this way: aroused, animated, imbued with the spirit to do a certain thing, by supernatural or divine influence.

What a "wow"! Another "wow" is the way the *American Heritage Dictionary* describes inspiration: to fill with noble and reverent emotion.

To demonstrate how empowering it is to carry with you noble thoughts and to deliver noble actions, I want to share with you a powerful truth from James Allen's 1904 classic *As a Man Thinketh*:

"The divinity that shapes our ends is in ourselves; it is our very self. And so we are held prisoners only by ourselves: Our own thoughts and actions are the jailors of our fate—they imprison, if they are base; they also are the angles of freedom—they liberate, if they are noble."

You see, an inspirational purpose—a resonating voice within—will always manifest noble and reverent emotions and forever liberate and set one free.

When I share with you how *Roget's College Thesaurus* describes "*motivation*" you will more than likely not say "Wow!" You would more than likely say, "Whoa, I didn't know that!" This is the description from the thesaurus on motivation:

- Induce
- Insight
- Provoke
- Instigate
- Bias
- Sway
- Tempt
- Seduce
- Bribe
- Enforce
- Impel
- Propel
- Whip
- Lash
- Goad

You see now why you would probably make me cry if you make reference to me as a great motivator. As we all know CPR resuscitates one's breathing. I want to be viewed as an inspirer—one who resuscitates another's emotions and in so doing create a new and different emotional dance.

The last description of motivation in *Roget's College Thesaurus* is this:

- An impulse to inspire.

I find this very interesting because motivation may take on the initial outward appearance of inspiration. It's not until you go on the inside that you see that motivation and inspiration are as different as darkness and light. Because of this, I see motivation as very deceptive in nature and it is an imposter to inspiration. When you think about it on a deeper level, motivation cannot even hold a candle to inspiration because it doesn't have the spiritual authenticity. Proverbs 20:27 states: "The spirit of man is the candle of the Lord . . ."

You see, motivation comes from man and the wants and will of man. Inspiration comes from God and the will of God being invited and welcomed to work through man. This is like comparing a *sole* proprietorship to a *soul* partnership.

What I discovered in my life is when you trade in your "go at it alone" sole proprietorship for a soul partnership, then you will find there is nothing more enlightening or empowering than when you partner with God. You will now find yourself standing at the daily floodgates of miracles; you will no longer have to exhaust yourself in an endless quest for meaning and significance. The law of attraction takes hold as never before; events, opportunities, and blessings flow to you easily, and ever increasingly.

If you were to build a new and beautiful house, wouldn't you go to a creative and competent architect so that you could be furnished with a *blueprint for success?* When you finally come to the crossroad of no longer wanting to live a life of quiet desperation and you are more than ready for a new and beautiful life, then why not go to the most creative and competent architect who ever has been or ever will be—the Architect of the Universe?

What I found to be true is that if you will *ask* then you will *receive* the most personalized *blueprint for success* that you could ever ask for or imagine. The Architect of the Universe will gladly and graciously furnish you with a newfound life and a newfound home. You will find that your newfound home's foundation will be built upon purpose. Its walls and rooms will resonate with voice and your beating heart will be housed with an endless sense of gratitude now that you've come home for the first and last time.

Motivation's emotional birthplace is in the mind of man, induced from thoughts, and grounded and anchored in a thing called the ego. The acronym EGO represents *Edging God Out.* Motivation is typically brought about at the expense of greed, fear, embarrassment, or guilt, and the end result is usually selfishness. What's in it for me, myself, and I?

Inspiration's emotional birthplace, on the other hand, is in the heart and it comes from the spirit, which induces feelings and emotions and its end result is not about selfishness but selflessness. It is not about me, myself, and I, but others. It is not about egotism but altruism. It's not about self above service but service above self.

In my life I've learned that goals are great but start with the heart before you live and give your part. By choosing to trust inspiration you will replace grunting, groaning, and speed bumps with hooting, hollering, and goose bumps. You will no longer be just living but you will now be *really* living for the first time.

Wright

Would you give our readers some further comparisons how the *way* of attaining results is so different from motivation and inspiration?

Douglas

Motivation	Inspiration
• Going through the motions.	Getting in the *flow*, if you know, what I mean.
• A wagon with a wobble.	A wagon.
• A round peg in a square hole. —*ouch!*	A round peg in a round hole —hmm! Feels good and feels right, because it is good and it is right.
• Making a dollar.	Making a difference.
• Transaction driven.	Client driven.
• Pushing for numbers.	Providing solutions to needs.
• Can't wait for Friday.	Can't wait for Monday, today, or any day.
• Pretender.	Surrender.

I don't think any of us know who the originator of the popular saying we hear so often today "thank God it's Friday" was, but I'm confident that people who say and emotionalize this are clearly not enjoying the wonder that a purpose-filled life provides.

A national statistic reveals the fact that suicide happens on Sunday evenings more than at any other time. This is right before what I call that voiceless, purposeless, Monday morning workweek grind. Another national statistic points out that heart attacks occur more often on Monday mornings... again, right before that voiceless, purposeless Monday morning workweek grind. I'm confident that if we had the ability to perform what I call an "emotional autopsy" on all those who committed suicide, we would discover that not one was living with purpose. The reason I make this confident statement is because, when you think about it, suicide is the epitome and the extreme act of selfishness. They only think of how to end their pain and are not concerned enough with the creation of the legacy of pain that their act will inflict upon their close friends and family who deeply care for and love them. I can honestly say that my Fridays do not have any more reverence or any more importance than my Mondays or any other day for that matter.

I love the saying, "Yesterday is history, tomorrow is a mystery, today is a gift, that is why they call it the *present*. People living with purpose are always in the moment—they are always in the now. They have a deep sense of gratitude because they reflect on each and every day as a wondrous gift. Their work is not really work at all—it is love, service, contribution, passion, and joy.

My last comparison between motivation and inspiration is *pretender* verses *surrender*. I view people who are living a purposeless life as great pretenders. I say this because they are not doing what they were created and designed to do, be, and become. For many years I identified surrender with weakness. What I found to be true is that in surrender lies our greatest strength. Surrender doesn't disempower but empowers one to new heights. It doesn't debilitate but it liberates and sets one free.

So with this in mind, I say: surrender the pretender so that it will no longer hinder either gender in being so blue (quiet desperation). Because when you surrender the pretender, what it will render is the most indescribable splendor because it will create the sweetest of sweet spots for you.

Wright

What is the sweetest of sweet spots?

Douglas

It is what I call living with *PURPOSE PIE*. My favorite pie is Mrs. Smith's Deep Dish Apple Pie. With all due respect to Mrs. Smith, the *PIE* I'm talking about is unlike any pie you've ever enjoyed. With this pie you don't have to worry about caloric intake, trans fat, fat grams, sugar, or cholesterol. With this pie you can consume as much as you like and it will never harm or hinder but it will only heal and render the sweetest of sweet spots.

When people with purpose sit daily at what I call the "table of life" and feast upon their purpose pie, it will do far more than just please their pallet. It will please their body, mind, heart, and spirit and it will please many who will cross their path in this wonderful thing we call life.

Wright

What are the ingredients that go into our purpose pie?

Douglas

There are three marvelous ingredients in our purpose pie.

- P—Passion: In the word *passion* you can find these three words crying to come out to serve others. These three words are: *"I pass on."* You see, people with voice and purpose are always passing on to others. They are always paying it forward in the form of service, contribution, care, and concern. When I reflect on passion I relate passion to pregnancy. With pregnancy you are not "kind of pregnant" or "a little pregnant"—you are either pregnant with child and life's full possibilities or you are not. The same thing works with passion. You never describe someone as "kind of passionate" because the person is either passion*ate* or passion*less*. People with purpose are unquestionably the most passionate people in the world. When you think about it, you either have an ". . .ate" at the end of your choice to live with passion or you have ". . . less" attached to the end of your choice to live without passion. People with purpose ate yesterday at the table of life and they are eating today from the table of life their purpose pie. Because of this, their "ATE" transforms into Always Touching Everyone.

  The passionless soul, on the other hand, knows far less about voice and purpose, in fact, most don't even have a clue. Their "LESS" transforms into Leaves Everyone Still and Silent. Remember, they are the ones who lead lives of quiet desperation. They leave others still and silent because their inner voice is still and silent.
- I—Inspiration: Inspiration is the second ingredient in our purpose pie. This is from the Latin word *"Inspirare"* meaning to breathe life into another.
- E—Enthusiasm. Enthusiasm is our third and last ingredient in our better than a blue ribbon winner pie. *Enthusiasm* comes from two Greek words: *en theos,* meaning in God, within God, inspired by God (there's that word again—"inspire"), or to breathe life into another. What really happens when you find your true, unique, and authentic purpose is that God is now breathing newfound life into

you. With His breath He fills you with the blessing of passion, inspiration, and enthusiasm. Now what has been created is what I call an ongoing, ever-flowing, motion of emotions. What you will then experience is that this ongoing, ever-flowing motion of emotions will be your constant companion 24/7, 365 days a year. It will be your trusted companion and remain with you until you take your . . . very . . . last . . . *breath*.

In reflecting on breath, I feel that far too many people put way too much energy and attention on the number of breaths we are fortunate enough to take in our lives. For me, the real significance should not be on the number of breaths we take but the number of moments and the number of experiences that we create within our life that take our breath away.

Purpose is the answer to this call because as you find your voice and inspire others to find their voice, you now breathe newfound life into another. It is in the giving and gifting of your purpose that your breath is taken away, but what you are left with is an indescribable sense of gratitude. Now you realize as never before you are no longer just living but *REALLY* living in the sweetest of sweet spots . . . "now that you've come home . . . for the first . . . and last time."

Wright

What a great conversation. I really appreciate the time you've taken to answer all these questions for me. I have really learned a lot. I think I've got a doctorate in purpose now and I owe it to you.

About the Author

STEVE DOUGLAS brings over thirty years of professional sales experience that involves three different industries. His clients have included professional athletes, universities, major corporations, manufacturers, and entrepreneurs alike. Steve has spoken to such groups as State Farm Insurance Companies, The Insurance & Financial Advisors Association for the State of Alaska, The National Association of Property Managers, and many athletic support events for the University of Florida.

Steve Douglas
6373 Highway 90
Milton, Florida 32570
Business: 850.623.0149
Cell: 850.748-6309
E-mail: steve@stevedouglas.org

Chapter Five

Kathleen Caldwell

David Wright (Wright)

Today we are talking with Kathleen Caldwell, one of the training and coaching profession's most popular and innovative consultants and speakers. Founder and president of Caldwell Consulting Group, Kathleen is a professional certified coach by The International Coach Federation. She is a member of the National Speakers Association and a consultant with more than twenty years of successful experience in senior management, sales, and marketing. Her company provides customized training and executive coaching programs for leading organizations. Her Fortune 1000 clients describe her as challenging, energetic, encouraging, and focused on results.

Her personal accomplishments include running two 26.2-mile marathons. Kathleen Caldwell welcome to *Blueprint for Success*.

Kathleen Caldwell (Caldwell)

Thank you for inviting me David. It is a pleasure to speak with you.

Wright

Kathleen, today we are talking about teamwork. You are a recognized expert with a successful training program in the area of team building. Do you have a working definition of teamwork that you apply to organizations?

Caldwell

Yes I do. After working with large and small companies for more than twenty years, I have found that teamwork is absolutely necessary for businesses to realize their true potential. Teamwork defines a group of people who have a common purpose, goals, and a structure for supporting each other to achieve the team's objectives. It fosters true employee engagement and loyalty, and that creates a work environment where everybody wins. Although it is not easy to do, when it works it is really outstanding.

Wright

You say that it is not easy to do. I really understand that. In my career, I have seen a lot of teams succeed and many fail. What would you say is the difference between teams that are really effective and those that aren't?

Caldwell

The teams that succeed are the ones whose members are aware, aligned, and committed. They are clear about the team's goals as well as their own purpose and role on the team.

I encourage people to ask themselves, "Why do I want to be employed by this company?" and, "Why do I want to be part of the team?" "How can my personal 'why' and 'win' be the connection and the investment I make in order to be successful and move the company forward?" Also, "What are my teammates' personal wins and whys for being on the team?"

These are only a sampling of the many questions and answers necessary to create a successful team and company. However, they are a great start in creating a corporate culture where everyone wins and Team Intelligence[SM] develops in the organization. In both small and large companies, when employees are clear about their own "why of our work," the "how to do it" becomes much easier.

I have professional sports teams as clients and I have discovered that most companies are like sports teams. Only an extraordinary team can win the Super Bowl or the World Series. The key is that everyone has a position on the team and each person performs it really, really well. The catcher doesn't try to be the pitcher, and the pitcher doesn't try to be the first baseman. The team members are clear about the rules of the game and their part in the team's success. They are also clear about their role on the team, their "why" and their teammates' "why" for winning.

Wright

Why is this so important for business and employees? Can't we keep doing things the same way we have always done them?

Caldwell

Of course; any organization can stay in the "business as usual" mode, but only if that business does not want to improve itself in all areas like increasing the bottom line, enhancing the work environment, and creating employee and customer loyalty.

David, there is a lot at stake for the future of business.

I see many teams that are not effective. I have worked with companies that have a lot of superstars and individual performers—people who were not invested in the organization's win. And the impact on business is tremendous. Even though superstar employees appear to be working together, they actually operate in their own self-imposed isolation, which they constantly reinforce. The end result is merely the appearance of teamwork that actually doesn't exist.

A subtle subversion occurs, and then resignation about the organization sets in. Employees begin to believe that it won't get any better and they mentally and emotionally "check out." Absenteeism, politics, and gossip increase and the business suffers. Resignation becomes almost like a virus spreading throughout an organization.

Obviously, these are not the goals of any business. So, what is at stake is a company's ability to reach a higher level of productivity, effectiveness, and competitiveness. What is possible is a new paradigm of business results, an environment of Team Intelligence, where people know their business purpose, they understand their roles, and execute them effectively. In this environment, clients are clear about what they can expect from the company and they operate out of a new spirit of partnership. What is possible is more creativity, connection, and communication among people. We can create organizations where people are not only invested in the company they work for, they are also invested in their teammates and clients in a brand new way. The results are really exciting!

Wright

I really believe that passion, expertise, and commitment are at the core of every successful businessperson. It is obvious that you have all of these qualities. Have you had the experience of teamwork in your business?

Caldwell

Oh, yes. Bringing true teamwork to my customers is really at the core of who I am as a businessperson. Creating teams that win is my company's purpose, and I have seen firsthand the difference between implementing Team Intelligence versus working alone in my own career and with my company. When I am collaborating with a team on a project, so much more is possible.

In my workshops, I ask participants to calculate how many uses there are for a single paper clip. When I have them do the exercise as individuals, they usually come up with four or five ideas. However, when I have them team up with others, they triple and quadruple the answers. Those results are what

I'm thinking of when I say, $1 + 1 = 3$. This is not bad math. 1 plus 1 will always equal 2, but 1 and 1 can team together and indeed create an additional 1 to equal 3. Transforming companies through this concept is my company's purpose. We are committed to it.

Wright

It is obvious that you are clear about your "why," and your company has had remarkable results with your clients. Congratulations.

Caldwell

David thanks for the compliment. This work is really rewarding!

Wright

You referred to a program called "Team Intelligence." That sounds interesting, tell us more about that.

Caldwell

"Team Intelligence" is a program that my company has developed from more than twenty years of experience working with companies and organizations both large and small. I researched companies that were not performing as planned and after studying the company's strategic plans, we analyzed the team to assess its ability to execute the plan and then reach its goals.

"Team Intelligence" is about bringing teams of people together more effectively. Our program is grounded in the premise that people inherently want to have a purpose for working, be connected, and work effectively with others; often they just don't know how to do that.

My company created the Team Intelligence program from research, surveys and client engagements. The program focuses on assessment, coaching, training, and consulting with a strong emphasis on assessment. We measure the progress and success of the curriculum by using DISC and 360-degree assessments and business scorecards.

Business scorecards are a lot like sports team scorecards. When you go to a baseball game, you see the managers and coaches working from the scorecard. They are evaluating the statistics of the players and how are they performing during the game and throughout the season. Then they use this information to give the players customized training, coaching, and a roadmap to success.

Team Intelligence employs a business scorecard system. The employee, team, and manager all work from the score card throughout the program to measure progress and success.

We have six steps in the Team Intelligence curriculum and score card system:

1. Effective Communication
2. Enhancing Trust
3. Designing Inspired Goals
4. Effectiveness and Accountability
5. Creating Extraordinary Relationships
6. Achieving Mastery

The first and fundamental step in Team Intelligence is creating *Effective Communication.* The most successful teams all have one basic ingredient in common: communication that is powerful, straight, and productive. Teams that are trained in powerful communication save time and resources, they avoid frustration and confusion, and ultimately, they are more productive. There is that old adage, "All problems exist in the absence of a good conversation."

The next step in the process is *Enhancing Trust.* From the Board of Directors to the entry-level employees, everyone in the organization is responsible for increasing and enhancing trust; within a team, this is critical. Trust is part of the foundation of creating an effective team. Trust creates an environment where team members have the confidence in the honesty, integrity, and reliability of each other. Each team member knows the others have his or her best interests at heart. Team members who trust one another can handle difficult issues and manage conflict with openness and ease. Through Team Intelligence, trust is not a random act; but instead, part of the core curriculum where it is learned, practiced, and coached.

The third step is *Designing Inspired Goals.* This section of the program defines the goals for the individual, the team, and the organization. What are we trying to accomplish? Do we have the right people on the team, doing the right things that are appropriate to their skills and strengths? We clarify how the individual's and team's goals align and interface.

The fourth step in Team Intelligence is *Effectiveness and Accountability.* Now that the team is clear about the goals, how do we execute the plan? What are the "rules of engagement" about working together—specifically around conflict resolution? What are the roles, values, and the responsibilities of the team members? For example, if it is my priority to leave work at 6:00 PM every day, no matter what, but my team's value is that we stay until the work is done, there's obvious conflict. Resolving that conflict is extremely important to getting the team aligned and in action.

And that leads me to step five, *Creating Extraordinary Relationships* at work. Now that the team is up and running, how do we manage conflict, operate at a higher level, and fortify partnerships with other teams within the organization and with our partners and clients?

Wright

This is really terrific. What is the last step?

Caldwell

That would be *Achieving Mastery*. This is where we put all of the components of the curriculum together. At this point in the program, the participants are actively and openly communicating with each other, operating in a more trusting environment, achieving inspiring goals, and creating extraordinary relationships. A spirit of partnership thrives in the organization and employees are enjoying their work. The company has engaged, loyal, and productive employees. When conflict occurs, as it always does, it is handled professionally and quickly. The team uses conflict to grow and expand the company, rather than as a divisive power tool. As a result, the organization is more profitable, competitive, innovative, and robust.

Wright

For companies that are already using teams or planning to use a team approach, why is Team Intelligence different?

Caldwell

Studies conducted by the American Society of Trainers and Developers (ASTD) indicates that 82 percent of companies in the United States already use teams. Traditional teamwork is not a new concept but Team Intelligence is a new methodology that adds structure and process for people to build trusting relationships, engage in a new way, and move beyond typical results.

In our research, we are finding that very few people still work for one manager at a time. Most employees now must work in teams to achieve greater results. We are working in a much more collaborative environment and in a global economy, so teaming effectively with others is absolutely critical.

Wright

That makes complete sense. What types of companies use Team Intelligence?

Caldwell

A wide variety of companies use Team Intelligence. Our clients span small technology companies with 200 employees to a large international food-manufacturing firm with tens of thousands of employees. We have also implemented Team Intelligence with a 600-employee National League baseball team.

The one thing our clients share is the common goal for their employees to work more effectively together and get the job done in a new way.

Wright

What have your clients told you about their results?

Caldwell

Their feedback is extraordinary. We frequently conduct surveys of past and current clients to assess the effectiveness of the Team Intelligence program. The results are impressive. Clients have reported:

"Trust is more present in our team. We're able to have conversations that were 'off limits' before the Team Intelligence program."

"Our team is working so much better together. We're actually creating healthy conflict so our group can grow and come up with new ideas. That wasn't happening before. We were stalled in our team's creativity and connection with each other."

"I am able to leave work at work mentally and physically. There is more balance in my life and I'm not worried about work in the evenings anymore. I get work issues handled right away and don't wait to have tough conversations about deadlines and problems."

"I am able to listen better without responding immediately and making snap judgments. I know that my teammates appreciate my new communication skills. Also, my wife thanks me for being more patient at home."

"Our team is so much more productive now. Our meeting time is now cut in half. We don't waste time arguing or explaining why we didn't get the work done; but instead, we get down to business right away, discuss the issues, create an action plan, assign responsibilities, and schedule our next meeting. I now have confidence that the people in my group will get their work done and let me know if problems arise. I don't feel left in the dark as before."

David, these are just a few examples of what my clients say about their results. I could list pages of testimonials, but essentially, people are reporting that they now operate at a new level. They are more "tuned in" with each other and with their clients, so their productivity and revenues increase. We find that Team Intelligence gives our clients the competitive edge.

Wright

Given all the news we have seen on television, heard on the radio, and read in the newspapers about American corporations trying to be more competitive and keep the trust of their employees and customers, this is a big thing and it is not going away.

Caldwell

Exactly. Trust in organizations inspires employees to take the initiative and be innovative. They can connect their own work purpose with the mission of the company and have the confidence that their work matters.

Team Intelligence creates a new culture of open communication and connection for employees. People report being more productive, focused, and they enjoy going to work. And that's the best measure of employee engagement and loyalty.

Wright

I have read statistics over and over again that anywhere from 40 percent to 87 percent of all of the people in America get up every morning and go to a place they don't want to be and do a job they don't like. Would you agree?

Caldwell

Oh, yes. I see that quite frequently in organizations. However, it does not have to be that way. I fundamentally believe that people want to be connected and have a purpose. They want to feel that their work makes a difference, that they are making a contribution to the advancement of the company and society as a whole. People want to enjoy their work and the people they are working with on a daily basis. The research indicates that dissatisfied employees do not leave companies—they leave bad managers and co-workers. If we can revive the sense of teamwork and connection in the workplace, we can dramatically reduce employee and client turnover.

Wright

You have been talking about the results team members are seeing. What do executives say the program does for them?

Caldwell

One of my clients is a technology healthcare company in the Midwest. *HR* magazine voted them one of the fifty best medium-sized companies to work for in America. Obviously, this is a prestigious honor. Even though this company is already successful, its executives still wanted to improve their teamwork and effectiveness. After working with a management team for only three months, the executives reported a dramatic increase in team engagement and focus, communication, healthy conflict, and trust. They said the most significant difference was finally knowing how to work together as a team rather than just as individuals coming together at random.

Executives tell me that they want a road map and process they can use that can be customized to their company's unique needs. They also want a partner that can see their situation clearly and objectively deliver a program. My clients also appreciate that I bring industry Best Practices to the engagement. They want to know what other successful companies are doing with teamwork and what they can do to compete.

Wright

What is possible for companies that implement Team Intelligence?

Caldwell

Well, David, the sky is the limit. The latest buzzwords in the Human Resource and Organizational Development fields are "Human Capital" and "Employee Engagement." Both terms sound rather theoretical, but they are about really utilizing employees and their intellectual expertise, passion, creativity, excitement, and commitment as a force within business.

When companies harness that incredible energy and momentum, who knows what is possible? We really cannot imagine the impact on society and the evolution of human kind, but I am sure that it could be really outstanding. This is a really enjoyable and exciting conversation to have and an extremely fulfilling way to conduct business. That is what I am committed to creating for businesses now and in the future.

Wright

You have been at this for more than twenty years. What is in the future for Kathleen?

Caldwell

I am working on several projects. With my husband, Michael Caldwell, I am co-authoring a book titled *Guilty or not Guilty? Are You Running Your Law Practice or Is Your Law Practice Running You?* We intend to show attorneys how to create a law practice that is fulfilling and super successful—on the lawyer's terms. Our book should be out in the first half of 2008. We are excited about it.

Wright

Why the interest in law? Is your husband in the legal profession?

Caldwell

Yes, Michael is a circuit court judge and before that he practiced law for more than thirty years. He has seen the challenges that lawyers have when their legal practice no longer works for them.

The American Bar Association has tracked some interesting trends. In one survey, upwards of 20 percent of lawyers admitted that they have a substance abuse problem, whether it is alcohol or drug abuse or a gambling problem. And this is something lawyers admitted voluntarily. Suicide and depression among male lawyers is approximately two times more likely than among men in the general population.

Now, we really do not know the full impact of substance abuse or depression in the legal community. However, there is another way. Michael and I believe that we can make a difference with lawyers by helping them to be aware of when their practice is running them, the effects of that, and how to choose a different course.

Wright

What a terrific and valuable book—not only for the lawyer, but also for the lawyer's partners, clients, and family.

Caldwell

Thank you, we think so too. We are also interviewing lawyers from all around the United States about how to run an effective practice. We hope to create a new paradigm about what is possible for the legal profession. This will be not only for lawyers but it will also be for judges, law students, and for society as a whole. Law touches every aspect of our daily life and we are thrilled about this book. We want to make a big difference!

Wright

What a great conversation! I really appreciate all the time you've taken to share your knowledge and experience with our readers and with me. I have learned some important information here today, and I am sure that our readers will appreciate learning more about you and your company.

Today we have been talking with Kathleen Caldwell. She is a coaching professional, certified by the International Coach Federation, and a member of the National Speakers Association. With more than twenty years of successful experience in consulting, senior management, sales and marketing, she founded and is and president of Caldwell Consulting Group.

Kathleen, thank you so much for being with us today on *Blueprint for Success.*

Caldwell

Thank you so much for the opportunity to speak with you. It has been wonderful.

About The Author

In the business of people and winning, Kathleen Caldwell inspires and coaches leaders and teams to perform to their ultimate potential. Kathleen brings over twenty years of experience winning in corporate management, sales, and marketing.

Known for her innovative, customized programs that truly deliver as promised, Kathleen is a popular speaker, keynote, executive coach, author, and consultant.

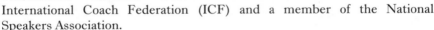

Kathleen received her coach training from the prestigious Coach University. She is a Professional Certified Coach with the International Coach Federation (ICF) and a member of the National Speakers Association.

Kathleen Caldwell and Caldwell Consulting Group, LLC will lead your team to *win!*

Kathleen Caldwell
Caldwell Consulting Group, LLC.
1482 White Oak Lane, Suite #1
Woodstock, IL 60098
815.206.4014
Kathleen@caldwellconsulting.biz
www.caldwellconsulting.biz

Chapter Six

An interview with…

Dr. Patricia Gangi

David Wright (Wright)

Today we are talking with Dr. Pat Gangi. We've heard so much about the cost of ethical failures in the workplace and it is clear that being unethical is not worth the cost. As a result, companies are now taking a closer look at the value of moral capital in their businesses.

Speaker and consultant Patricia A. Gangi, EDD, is an advocate for ethical champions in the workplace. Dr. Gangi has been working with companies and government entities for more than twenty years to create work environments that support and encourage ethical treatment of both internal and external customers. She talks here today about the role of ethical champions and about raising the level of ethical commitment in the workplace.

Dr. Gangi, welcome to *Blueprint for Success.*

Dr. Pat Gangi (Gangi)

Thank you, David.

Wright

Some say that in today's highly competitive and tightly regulated workplace, businesses can't succeed without leaders bending the rules a bit. Do you agree?

Gangi

No, I don't. Those who think that way probably define success in the narrow sense of achieving certain numbers or reaching a particular endpoint. It doesn't matter how they get there or how much road-kill they leave behind as long as they meet or exceed their profit goals.

Society is changing; people are demanding that companies and individual leaders not only hit their numbers but do so ethically and in a way that is socially, economically, and environmentally sensitive. It is not just the endpoint that counts now—it is the means to that end as well.

The good news is that acting ethically can have great positive impact on both the business and the individual employee. For example, the Josephson Ethics Institute's report on *The Hidden Costs of Unethical Behavior* found that ethical firms have lower turnover rates. Ethically run businesses tend to retain employees with important skills. They also waste less time training their employees and attract top-flight talent more easily. And, employees want to stay at a company with a positive ethical environment. It short, a highly ethical work environment translates into reduced expenditures for the business in terms of recruiting, hiring, and training and a more motivating and rewarding work environment for the employee.

Wright

Everyone has some sense of what ethics are, so how do you define ethics?

Gangi

I define *ethics* as the set of behaviors we choose to support our *core values*. Core values are those basic principles we believe are most important in our lives and in our work.

For example, if I value fairness, then my personal ethic might include behaviors such as always listening to both sides of a story and not prejudging a situation because of someone's prior actions. In a work context, if a business has a core value of fairness then supervisors would not play favorites and would provide staff members with timely and evenhanded performance evaluations.

When we talk about people *acting ethically* we are saying that their behaviors are consistent with the values they hold. As an ethical employee, my actions should align with my company's core values. Hopefully my personal values and the organization's values are compatible. If not I'm bound to find the work challenging at best and unbearable at worst.

Wright

You talk about a need to move beyond compliance in workplace ethics. Would you tell the readers what you mean by that?

Gangi

The well-publicized business scandals of recent years and the inability or unwillingness of the private sector to clean up its own house led the government to step in and institute laws and regulations such as the Sarbanes-Oxley Act of 2002, also known as SOX. SOX requires businesses to—among other things—adopt certain governance rules, meet increased reporting requirements, demonstrate greater accountability, establish ethics codes, conduct ethics training, and add hotlines for employees to report unethical behavior.

Because of the onerous penalties mandated by SOX for not complying with the paperwork-heavy regulations, many more companies now have an ethics code and take a stab at some type of ethics training so they can be considered compliant with SOX. However, law has both letter and spirit. Having a code might meet the letter of the law—in other words, the company may be technically compliant—but if the code stays framed on the wall and has little, if any, real impact on the way the company conducts business, then it fails to obey the spirit of the law.

Many of the businesses involved in the scandals, including Enron, already had ethics codes and provided some level of ethics training to their employees, yet the corruption still occurred. Why? I think it's because the codes and training activities were treated as "window-dressing"—passive actions designed to be raised as part of a "reasonable-efforts" defense should someone be caught. *These companies did little, if anything, to create a positive, proactive ethical environment in which ethical behavior was encouraged, acknowledged, and celebrated.*

In such an environment, leaders live the company's core values, the ethics code serves as a dynamic guideline for conducting business, and employees are encouraged to become ethical champions. Without a toxic, negative atmosphere, employees are more willing to challenge unethical behavior and eventually the negative behaviors are crowded out.

Wright

You promote the development of ethical champions in business. Would you tell me more about that?

Gangi

As we both know, David, the workplace can be quite challenging and it takes champions—people willing to stand up for what's right—to change an unethical work culture.

This is a particularly difficult challenge for newer workers just coming out of high school or college. A 2002 report by the Josephson Ethics Institute found that 74 percent of high school students admitted to cheating on at least one exam in the previous year. That figure is up from 61 percent in 1992.

Perhaps a greater indicator is that more than 50 percent agreed with the statement: "A person has to lie or cheat sometimes to get ahead." Why do they believe this? The pressure to succeed in school is often intense and competitive, and technological advances such as cell phones and wireless Internet access have made it easier to cheat. Because a significant number of students do succumb to cheating, those who would not normally act unethically feel as if they have no choice—their hard work no longer provides a competitive advantage. Many of these young workers believe that the workplace holds more of the same—they won't be able to succeed unless they cheat to balance the playing field.

It's even more troubling to know that most adults don't think reporting unethical behavior is going to make a difference. A recent report by the Ethics Resource Center and The Society for Human Resource Management found that 65 percent of working adults do nothing when they see something illegal or unethical in the workplace.

This is why we need ethical champions. Ethical champions are those who stay faithful to their core values. They are role models and leaders who motivate ethical followers by encouragement and example, not by threats and intimidation. They play by the rules but also respond to the spirit of the law. Ethical champions also understand that just because you *can* do something (you have the legal authority or right to do it) doesn't always mean you *should* do something. Ethical champions do the right things even when it could cost them their jobs and their reputations.

Wright

So, I guess that doing the right things is not always as easy as one might think it is!

Gangi

You're right, and I know this from personal experience. Acting ethically, while personally satisfying, can be very costly. A number of years ago, after eight frustrating months of unemployment in a very tight economy, I finally landed a short-term contract to survey and report on the progress of a small college's federal grant program. When the program director saw the mixed and unflattering results, he directed me to falsify the report by submitting only the positive data. He implied that I would lose a promised contract extension if I refused to do so.

I wish I could say it was an easy call to do the right thing, but it wasn't. I was very tempted to go along with the false report so I could continue to work; being out of work for such a long time had been so difficult! I struggled with it for a time, but finally my conscience (that inner knowledge I we all have deep inside about what is right and what is wrong) finally won out. I refused the director's order. I think my response took him by surprise because he backed off and allowed me to submit an accurate report. However, he also rescinded the contract extension and in no time at all I was back on the unemployment line. At least my soul was intact!

Wright

What do you think are the biggest obstacles to becoming an ethical champion in the workplace?

Gangi

I think there are two big obstacles. First, employees may have a narrow perspective on work and second, they may have an immature commitment to ethical action.

In terms of perspective, there are three common ways to look at work:
1. Work as "just a job"
2. Work as an all-consuming career
3. Work as a vocation

Those who think of work solely as a job tend to have a *pocketbook perspective*. They work to pay the bills. Their work simply supports the other, more important parts of their life. People with this mindset often under-invest in their work, doing just what's needed to get by or to pay the next bill.

I heard a great example of this the other day. A friend who owns a small restaurant hired a new food server. The employee's work was okay, but not great. One day after working just three hours of her six-hour shift, the employee approached my friend and asked if she could go home. Concerned, he asked if she was feeling ill. "No, I'm fine. I just needed to make twenty-five dollars today and I did that already, so I want to go home now." She showed absolutely no concern for her work beyond her paycheck. Amazing, isn't it?

People who consider work "just a job" often do the bare minimum required to keep the paychecks coming. They also tend to live ethically on the edge, willing to compromise their ethical values when it means more money.

Next, we have those who think of work entirely as a career. These are the workaholics, who over-invest in their jobs, putting in eighteen-hour days and not understanding why everyone else isn't as committed. They define themselves by their work and may, at times, compromise their ethics to move their careers forward.

The third way of looking at work is as a *vocation*. This is the most balanced of the three approaches and the one with more meaning and impact. Someone who sees work as a vocation says, "Yes, I do need to work to pay my bills and I do want a career, but I also see my work as an opportunity to make a meaningful contribution to society." When work is seen as a vocation, employees find deep personal satisfaction even from very difficult work because they recognize how their efforts make a difference. Those who see work as a vocation experience a certain satisfaction that enables them to make the hard but right ethical choices when confronted in the workplace.

So, one can overcome the first major obstacle to becoming an ethical champion by choosing to look at work as a vocation. The second major obstacle is having an immature ethical commitment.

We can look at ethics at three levels of maturity: *Containment*, *Consequence*, and *Congruence*. The least mature stage is the *Containment* level, or the "toddler approach" to ethics. At this level, the employee says, "I don't steal because the boss locks the supply room door—I'm not unethical because the company doesn't give me the opportunity to be unethical." There is really no moral choice involved at this level because it is not possible for the employee to be unethical. It's akin to confining toddlers to a playpen so they can't get into trouble.

The second level of ethical maturity is the *Consequence* level, or what I refer to as the "teenage approach" to ethics. "I don't steal because there is a punishment for stealing or a reward for not stealing." It's like telling a teenager, "Okay, son [or daughter], I will give you the car keys, but if you get a ticket, you're grounded for three months." Or, "If you stay accident-free and ticket-free this whole year, I will pay your car insurance next year." At this level, people act ethically due to external consequences of either getting a reward or avoiding a punishment.

At the mature level of commitment, the *Congruence* level, the individual says, "I don't steal because I know myself and I am not a thief! I know what I stand for, I know my core beliefs, and make sure my actions are congruent or aligned with those beliefs." The person acts with integrity, with wholeness. The motivation is intrinsic, coming from the inside and moving out; decisions don't depend on anyone else. It does, however, demand that people take time to reflect on who they are and what they believe at their core.

Wright

What ethical champions have influenced you in your work and studies?

Gangi

My heroes are those who have shown great moral courage by speaking up even when they knew they would suffer significant retaliation. I'm talking about people like whistle-blower Sharon Watson, an Enron employee whose decision to share her ethical concerns broke open the Enron scandal. I also admire two brave FBI agents who experienced severe retaliation including harassment and dismissal after reporting several of their FBI co-workers for stealing items from Ground Zero for souvenirs. These objects may have included personal items belonging to September 11 victims. As someone born and raised in New York, I find their ethical courage to be a bright light against the darkness of that tragic event.

One of my favorite ethical champions is a grandmother here in Arizona who recently discovered that her grandson had committed a felony hit-and-run accident. He mentioned it to her and she immediately marched him to the nearest police station. Even though she knew he would end up in prison, she wouldn't cover up for him. She would not stand for it; the family has a long-standing core value of accepting responsibility for their actions, good or bad, and he needed to live by the family's ethical code. Deep down, the grandson knew she was right and didn't fight her decision.

These are my heroes, the everyday people who step out and do what's right even when the consequences are difficult.

Wright

You mentioned the word whistle-blower. It sounds so negative in our culture that even doing the right thing one is still chastised by society.

Gangi

That is why I like to call them ethical champions. They are, in many cases, real heroes because they do put their lives, their reputations, and their careers on the line in support of ethical behavior. I think it's a great idea to change that negative perception by referring to whistle-blowers as ethical champions.

Wright

When companies don't have meaningful ethics codes or standards of employee conduct, how can well-intentioned employees make good ethical decisions?

Gangi

I would suggest that they follow a decision-making guide. Let me recommend a simple guide that has three questions: Is the behavior you are contemplating compliant? Is it considerate? Is it consistent?

- *Is it compliant?*

As far as you can tell without having access to the actual written documents, does the behavior seem to be legal and follow standard policy and procedure?

- *Is it considerate?*

How does this behavior choice impact others? What if your parents, children, co-workers, or friends read about this on the front page of the biggest newspaper in town or saw it on the nightly news or U-Tube? Would you be proud of it?

Who will suffer by the decision and who will benefit in the long- and short-term?

Here is an example: Let's say you are a manager who set his team's vacation schedule at the beginning of the year. You later find out that Tiger Woods is going to play a golf tournament in your city. You are a golf fanatic and Tiger Woods is your hero, so you change the vacation schedule to enable you to attend the tournament.

In the short-term who benefits? You do. But what about the long-term view? What about the employee whose vacation you've switched? Perhaps it was the week of her daughter's wedding and now she has to take leave without pay in order to get the time off. What is that going to do to the long-term relationship with your employees? You can't look at this decision in isolation. You need to ask, "Who is it going to impact, short- term *and* long-term."

- *Is it consistent?*

Is the action you are about to take consistent with the truth—is it honest? Is it the whole truth? The problem that I was faced with when asked by my director to falsify the report wasn't one of dishonesty. The figures we were submitting were true, but they weren't the *whole* truth. It was dishonest by omission.

Does the behavior align with both your personal and organizational values? Is it consistent with actions you've taken in the past? Employees often call decisions arbitrary or unethical when those decisions are inconsistent from one situation or person to the next.

Does the behavior avoid even the appearance of unethical behavior? Could you sleep at night with a clear conscience? I love this anonymous quote: *"Your conscience is like a baby; it has to go to sleep before you can."*

Wright

What can companies do to ensure that their ethics program serves a meaningful purpose rather than just lie on a shelf like a dead document?

Gangi

Many employees tend to be cynical or skeptical when a company starts to implement an ethics program. We hear statements like:

- "Oh, so now you're implementing a program that treats me like an infant and assumes I don't know right from wrong."
- "You're proposing a path for me that you don't walk yourself."
- "This is just the latest program of the month."

I think you can minimize a great many of these negative attitudes if you grow this program from the bottom up. That means incorporating employees' ideas and ideals. Include representatives from all the different employee levels or groups (executive, management, line staff, day shift, night shift, etc.) when developing the organization's ethical guidelines and ethics training programs. When employees believe they have a stake in the process, when they see their own values represented in the guidelines, they are usually more open to receiving them and responding to them positively.

I also think it is a good idea to use a team-teaching approach: have a respected member of top management team up with a respected employee representative to deliver ethics training.

Wright

If you were going to encourage someone to develop one key skill that would help him or her become an ethical champion what would that be?

Gangi

Without a doubt it would be the skill of critical reflection. According to the *Harvard Business Review* it is one of the key skills of successful managers, yet it is practiced by fewer than 10 percent of the management population. Managers tend to be very good at analysis but terrible at reflection.

Let me give you an example of how analysis differs from reflection. An analyst might look at a sunset and describe it this way: "Sunset, also called sundown, occurs when the sun drops below the horizon. At that time you may see red light. This is caused by a combination of light refraction and dust particles in the atmosphere."

How does a reflective person describe a sunset? *"...Wow!"*

You see, David, one is information and the other is appreciation. I think we need both. We need to collect and analyze data to make good decisions about how to act; but we also need to reflect and consider the issues we discussed at the very beginning of our conversation: the social, economic, environmental, and ethical impact of those same decisions.

Wright

What message would you like to leave with our readers as being crucial to building an environment where ethics are a first thought and not an afterthought?

Gangi

The message is this: what do you want leave as your ethical legacy? Someday you are going to leave the company you're with now to take another position or perhaps to retire. How do you want to be remembered by your colleagues? How do you want to be remembered by your family and friends? That is a powerful consideration.

You may have heard of J. Clifford Baxter, a former Enron VP deeply enmeshed in the scandal, who chose to commit suicide. In his suicide note Mr. Baxter indicated that he couldn't live with the pain anymore: "I have always tried to do the right thing, but where there was once great pride, now it's gone." He was saddened by the darkness of his legacy to the point of taking his own life. Unfortunately, he also deprived himself of any way to redeem that legacy, but that's another issue.

What is the legacy you want to leave? How do you want to be remembered? This powerful consideration can motivate you to always do the right thing, even when no one is looking.

Wright

What a great session. I really appreciate your answering all these questions. These are important and will make our *Blueprint for Success* book much better by having talked about ethics.

Today we have been talking with Dr. Pat Gangi, speaker and consultant. She is an advocate for ethical champions in the workplace. Dr. Gangi has been working with companies and government for over twenty years to create work environments that support and encourage ethical treatment, both internal and external.

Dr. Gangi, thank you so much for being with us today on *Blueprint for Success*.

Gangi

And thank you, David, especially for letting me speak so freely about my passion!

About the Author

DR. PATRICIA GANGI has more than twenty years' experience creating highly customized learning programs for public and private sector clients. After earning her doctorate in instructional design from Arizona State University, Dr. Pat completed the Public Sector Ethics program at the renowned Josephson Institute of Ethics. Dr. Pat focuses on workplace ethics, coaching, and emotionally intelligent customer service. An experienced facilitator, she often leads training workshops, business retreats, and strategic planning sessions. Her clients include Honeywell Aerospace, Loews Hotels & Resorts, Pinnacle Entertainment, and numerous public sector agencies. Dr. Pat is an active professional member of the National Speakers Association and an award-winning Distinguished Toastmaster.

Dr. Patricia Gangi
Cornerstone International
1628 E. Southern Ave., Ste. 9 PMB-327
Tempe, AZ 85282
480.730.1010
www.cornerstone-intl.com

Chapter Seven

An interview with...

Dr. Kenneth Blanchard

David E. Wright (Wright)

Few people have created a positive impact on the day-to-day management of people and companies more than Dr. Kenneth Blanchard. He is known around the world simply as Ken, a prominent, gregarious, sought-after author, speaker, and business consultant. Ken is universally characterized by friends, colleagues, and clients as one of the most insightful, powerful, and compassionate men in business today. Ken's impact as a writer is far-reaching. His phenomenal best-selling book, *The One Minute Manager*®, co-authored with Spencer Johnson, has sold more than thirteen million copies worldwide and has been translated into more than twenty-five languages. Ken is Chairman and "Chief Spiritual Officer" of the Ken Blanchard Companies. The organization's focus is to energize organizations around the world with customized training in bottom-line business strategies based on the simple, yet powerful principles inspired by Ken's best-selling books.

Dr. Blanchard, welcome to *Blueprint for Success*.

Dr. Ken Blanchard (Blanchard)

Well, it's nice to talk with you, David. It's good to be here.

Wright

I must tell you that preparing for your interview took quite a bit more time than usual. The scope of your life's work and your business, the Ken Blanchard Companies, would make for a dozen fascinating interviews.

Before we dive into the specifics of some of your projects and strategies, will you give our readers a brief synopsis of your life—how you came to be the Ken Blanchard we all know and respect?

Blanchard

Well, I'll tell you, David, I think life is what you do when you are planning on doing something else. I think that was John Lennon's line. I never intended to do what I have been doing. In fact, all my professors in college told me that I couldn't write. I wanted to do college work, which I did, and they said, "You had better be an administrator." So I decided I was going to be a Dean of Students. I got provisionally accepted into my master's degree program and then provisionally accepted at Cornell because I never could take any of those standardized tests.

I took the college boards four times and finally got 502 in English. I don't have a test-taking mind. I ended up in a university in Athens, Ohio, in 1966 as an Administrative Assistant to the Dean of the Business School. When I got there he said, "Ken, I want you to teach a course. I want all my deans to teach." I had never thought about teaching because they said I couldn't write, and teachers had to publish. He put me in the manager's department.

I've taken enough bad courses in my day and I wasn't going to teach one. I really prepared and had a wonderful time with the students. I was chosen as one of the top ten teachers on the campus coming out of the chute!

I just had a marvelous time. A colleague by the name of Paul Hersey was chairman of the Management Department. He wasn't very friendly to me initially because the Dean had led me to his department, but I heard he was a great teacher. He taught Organizational Behavior and Leadership. So I said, "Can I sit in on your course next semester?"

"Nobody audits my courses," he said. "If you want to take it for credit, you're welcome."

I couldn't believe it. I had a doctoral degree and he wanted me to take his course for credit—so I signed up.

The registrar didn't know what to do with me because I already had a doctorate, but I wrote the papers and took the course, and it was great.

In June 1967, Hersey came into my office and said, "Ken, I've been teaching in this field for ten years. I think I'm better than anybody, but I can't write. I'm a nervous wreck, and I'd love to write a textbook with somebody. Would you write one with me?"

I said, "We ought to be a great team. You can't write and I'm not supposed to be able to, so let's do it!"

Thus began this great career of writing and teaching. We wrote a textbook called *Management of Organizational Behavior: Utilizing Human Resources*. It came out in its eighth edition October 3, 2000 and the ninth edition was published September 3, 2007. It has sold more than any other textbook in that area over the years. It's been over forty years since that book first came out.

I quit my administrative job, became a professor, and ended up working my way up the ranks. I got a sabbatical leave and went to California for one year twenty-five years ago. I ended up meeting Spencer Johnson at a cocktail party. He wrote children's books— wonderful series called *Value Tales® for Kids*. He also wrote *The Value of Courage: The Story of Jackie Robinson* and *The Value of Believing In Yourself: The Story Louis Pasteur*.

My wife, Margie, met him first and said, "You guys ought to write a children's book for managers because they won't read anything else." That was my introduction to Spencer. So, *The One Minute Manager* was really a kid's book for big people. That is a long way from saying that my career was well planned.

Wright

Ken, what and/or who were your early influences in the areas of business, leadership, and success? In other words, who shaped you in your early years?

Blanchard

My father had a great impact on me. He was retired as an admiral in the Navy and had a wonderful philosophy. I remember when I was elected as president of the seventh grade, and I came home all pumped up. My father said, "Son, it's great that you're the president of the seventh grade, but now that you have that leadership position, don't ever use it." He said, "Great leaders are followed because people respect them and like them, not because they have power." That was a wonderful lesson for me early on. He was just a great model for me. I got a lot from him.

Then I had this wonderful opportunity in the mid 1980s to write a book with Norman Vincent Peale. He wrote *The Power of Positive Thinking*. I met him when he was eighty-six years old; we were asked to write a book on ethics together, *The Power of Ethical Management: Integrity Pays, You Don't Have to Cheat to Win*. It didn't matter what we were writing together, I learned so much from him. He just built from the positive things I learned from my mother.

My mother said that when I was born I laughed before I cried; I danced before I walked, and I smiled before I frowned. So that, as well as Norman Vincent Peale, really impacted me as I focused on what I could do to train leaders. How do you make them positive? How do you make them realize that it's not about them, it's about who they are serving? It's not about their position—it's about what they can do to help other people win.

So, I'd say my mother and father, then Norman Vincent Peale. All had a tremendous impact on me.

Wright

I can imagine. I read a summary of your undergraduate and graduate degrees. I assumed you studied Business Administration, marketing management, and related courses. Instead, at Cornell you studied Government and Philosophy. You received your master's from Colgate in Sociology and Counseling and your PhD from Cornell in Educational Administration and Leadership. Why did you choose this course of study? How has it affected your writing and consulting?

Blanchard

Well, again, it wasn't really well planned out. I originally went to Colgate to get a master's degree in Education because I was going to be a Dean of Students over men. I had been a Government major, and I was a Government major because it was the best department at Cornell in the Liberal Arts School. It was exciting. We would study what the people were doing at the league of governments. And then, the Philosophy Department was great. I just loved the philosophical arguments. I wasn't a great student in terms of getting grades, but I'm a total learner. I would sit there and listen, and I would really soak it in.

When I went over to Colgate and got into the education courses, they were awful. They were boring. The second week, I was sitting at the bar at the Colgate Inn saying, "I can't believe I've been here two years for this." This is just the way the Lord works: Sitting next to me in the bar was a young sociology professor who had just gotten his PhD at Illinois. He was staying at the Inn. I was moaning and groaning about what I was doing, and he said, "Why don't you come and major with me in sociology? It's really exciting."

"I can do that?" I asked.

He said, "Yes."

I knew they would probably let me do whatever I wanted the first week. Suddenly, I switched out of Education and went with Warren Ramshaw. He had a tremendous impact on me. He retired some years ago as the leading professor at Colgate in the Arts and Sciences, and got me interested in leadership and organizations. That's why I got a master's in Sociology.

The reason I went into educational administration and leadership? It was a doctoral program I could get into because I knew the guy heading up the program. He said, "The greatest thing about Cornell is that you will be in the School of Education. It's not very big, so you don't have to take many education courses, and you can take stuff all over the place."

There was a marvelous man by the name of Don McCarty who eventually became the Dean of the School of Education, Wisconsin. He had an impact on my life; but I was always just searching around.

My mission statement is: to be a loving teacher and example of simple truths that help myself and others to awaken the presence of God in our lives. The reason I mention "God" is that I believe the biggest addiction in the world is the human ego; but I'm really into simple truth. I used to tell people I was trying to get the B.S. out of the behavioral sciences.

Wright

I can't help but think, when you mentioned your father, that he just bottom-lined it for you about leadership.

Blanchard

Yes.

Wright

A man named Paul Myers, in Texas, years and years ago when I went to a conference down there, said, "David, if you think you're a leader and you look around, and no one is following you, you're just out for a walk."

Blanchard

Well, you'd get a kick out of this—I'm just reaching over to pick up a picture of Paul Myers on my desk. He's a good friend, and he's a part of our Center for Faith Walk Leadership where we're trying to challenge and equip people to lead like Jesus. It's non-profit. I tell people I'm not an evangelist because we've got enough trouble with the Christians we have. We don't need any more new ones. But, this is a picture of Paul on top of a mountain. Then there's another picture below that of him under the sea with stingrays. It says, "Attitude is everything. Whether you're on the top of the mountain or the bottom of the sea, true happiness is achieved by accepting God's promises, and by having a biblically positive frame of mind. Your attitude is everything." Isn't that something?

Wright

He's a fine, fine man. He helped me tremendously. In keeping with the theme of our book, *Blueprint for Success,* I wanted to get a sense from you about your own success journey. Many people know you best from *The One Minute Manager* books you coauthored with Spencer Johnson. Would you consider these books as a high water mark for you or have you defined success for yourself in different terms?

Blanchard

Well, you know, *The One Minute Manager* was an absurdly successful book so quickly that I found I couldn't take credit for it. That was when I really got on my own spiritual journey and started to try to find out what the real meaning of life and success was.

That's been a wonderful journey for me because I think, David, the problem with most people is they think their self-worth is a function of their performance plus the opinion of others. The minute you think that is what your self-worth is, every day your self-worth is up for grabs because your performance is going to fluctuate on a day-to-day basis. People are fickle. Their opinions are going to go up and down. You need to ground your self-worth in the unconditional love that God has ready for us, and that really grew out of the unbelievable success of *The One Minute Manager*.

When I started to realize where all that came from, that's how I got involved in this ministry that I mentioned. Paul Myers is a part of it. As I started to read the Bible, I realized that everything I've ever written about, or taught, Jesus did. You know, He did it with the twelve incompetent guys He "hired." The only guy with much education was Judas, and he was His only turnover problem.

Wright

Right.

Blanchard

This is a really interesting thing. What I see in people is not only do they think their self-worth is a function of their performance plus the opinion of others, but they measure their success on the amount of accumulation of wealth, on recognition, power, and status. I think those are nice success items. There's nothing wrong with those, as long as you don't define your life by that.

What I think you need to focus on rather than success is what Bob Buford, in his book *Halftime,* calls "significance"—moving from success to significance. I think the opposite of accumulation of wealth is generosity.

I wrote a book called *The Generosity Factor* with Truett Cathy who is the founder of Chick-fil-A. He is one of the most generous men I've ever met in my life. I thought we needed to have a model of generosity. It's not only your *treasure,* but it's your *time* and *talent.* Truett and I added *touch* as a fourth one.

The opposite of recognition is service. I think you become an adult when you realize you're here to serve rather than to be served.

Finally, the opposite of power and status is loving relationships. Take Mother Teresa as an example—she couldn't have cared less about recognition, power, and status because she was focused on generosity, service, and loving relationships; but she got all of that earthly stuff. If you focus on the earthly, such as money, recognition, and power, you're never going to get to significance. But if you focus on significance, you'll be amazed at how much success can come your way.

Wright

I spoke with Truett Cathy recently and was impressed by what a down-to-earth, good man he seems to be. When you start talking about him closing his restaurants on Sunday, all of my friends—when they found out I had talked to him—said, "Boy, he must be a great Christian man, but he's rich." I told them, "Well, to put his faith into perspective, by closing on Sunday it costs him $500 million a year."

He lives his faith, doesn't he?

Blanchard

Absolutely, but he still outsells everybody else.

Wright

That's right.

Blanchard

According to their January 25, 2007, press release, Chick-fil-A was the nation's second-largest quick-service chicken restaurant chain in sales at that time. Its business performance marks the thirty-ninth consecutive year the chain has enjoyed a system-wide sales gain—a streak the company has sustained since opening its first chain restaurant in 1967.

Wright

The simplest market scheme, I told him, tripped me up. I walked by his first Chick-fil-A I had ever seen, and some girl came out with chicken stuck on toothpicks and handed me one; I just grabbed it and ate it, it's history from there on.

Blanchard

Yes, I think so. It's really special. It is so important that people understand generosity, service, and loving relationships because too many people are running around like a bunch of peacocks. You even see pastors who measure their success by how many in are in their congregation; authors by how many books they have sold; businesspeople by what their profit margin is—how good sales are. The reality is that's all well and good, but I think what you need to focus on is the other. I think if business did that more and we got Wall Street off our backs with all the short-term evaluation, we'd be a lot better off.

Wright

Absolutely. There seems to be a clear theme that winds through many of your books that have to do with success in business and organizations—how people are treated by management and how they feel about their value to a company. Is this an accurate observation? If so, can you elaborate on it?

Blanchard

Yes, it's a very accurate observation. See, I think the profit is the applause you get for taking care of your customers and creating a motivating environment for your people. Very often people think that business is only about the bottom line. But no, that happens to be the result of creating raving fan customers, which I've described with Sheldon Bowles in our book, *Raving Fans*. Customers want to brag about you, if you create an environment where people can be gung-ho and committed. You've got to take care of your customers and your people, and then your cash register is going to go ka-ching, and you can make some big bucks.

Wright

I noticed that your professional title with the Ken Blanchard Companies is somewhat unique—"Chairman and Chief Spiritual Officer." What does your title mean to you personally and to your company? How does it affect the books you choose to write?

Blanchard

I remember having lunch with Max DuPree one time. The legendary Chairman of Herman Miller, Max wrote a wonderful book called *Leadership Is an Art*.

"What's your job?" I asked him.

He said, "I basically work in the vision area."

"Well, what do you do?" I asked.

"I'm like a third grade teacher," he replied. "I say our vision and values over, and over, and over again until people get it right, right, right."

I decided from that, I was going to become the Chief Spiritual Officer, which means I would be working in the vision, values, and energy part of our business. I ended up leaving a morning message every day for everybody in our company. We have twenty-eight international offices around the world.

I leave a voice mail every morning, and I do three things on that as Chief Spiritual Officer: One, people tell me who we need to pray for. Two, people tell me who we need to praise—our unsung heroes and people like that. And then three, I leave an inspirational morning message. I really am the cheerleader—the Energizer Bunny—in our company. I'm the reminder of why we're here and what we're trying to do.

We think that our business in the Ken Blanchard Companies is to help people lead at a higher level, and to help individuals and organizations. Our mission statement is to unleash the power and potential of people and organizations for the common good. So if we are going to do that, we've really got to believe in that.

I'm working on getting more Chief Spiritual Officers around the country. I think it's a great title and we should get more of them.

Wright

So those people for whom you pray, where do you get the names?

Blanchard

The people in the company tell me who needs help, whether it's a spouse who is sick or kids who are sick or if they are worried about something. We've got over five years of data about the power of prayer, which is pretty important.

One morning, my inspirational message was about my wife and five members of our company who walked sixty miles one weekend—twenty miles a day for three days—to raise money for breast cancer research.

It was amazing. I went down and waved them all in as they came. They had a ceremony; they had raised 7.6 million dollars. There were over three thousand people walking. A lot of the walkers were dressed in pink—they were cancer victors—people who had overcome it. There were even men walking with pictures of their wives who had died from breast cancer. I thought it was incredible.

There wasn't one mention about it in the major San Diego papers. I said, "Isn't that just something." We have to be an island of positive influence because all you see in the paper today is about celebrities and their bad behavior. Here you have all these thousands of people out there walking and trying to make a difference, and nobody thinks it's news.

So every morning I pump people up about what life is about, about what's going on. That's what my Chief Spiritual Officer job is about.

Wright

I had the pleasure of reading one of your releases, *The Leadership Pill*.

Blanchard

Yes.

Wright

I must admit that my first thought was how short the book was. I wondered if I was going to get my money's worth, which by the way, I most certainly did. Many of your books are brief and based on a fictitious story. Most business books in the market today are hundreds of pages in length and are read almost like a textbook.

Will you talk a little bit about why you write these short books, and about the premise of *The Leadership Pill?*

Blanchard

I really developed my relationship with Spencer Johnson when we wrote *The One Minute Manager*. As you know, he wrote, *Who Moved My Cheese*, which was a phenomenal success. He wrote children's books and is quite a storyteller.

Jesus taught by parables, which were short stories.

My favorite books are, *Jonathan Livingston Seagull* and *The Little Prince*.

Og Mandino, author of seventeen books, was the greatest of them all.

I started writing parables because people can get into the story and learn the contents of the story, and they don't bring their judgmental hats into reading. You write a regular book and they'll say, "Well, where did you get the research?" They get into that judgmental side. Our books get them emotionally involved and they learn.

The Leadership Pill is a fun story about a pharmaceutical company that thinks they have discovered the secret to leadership, and they can put the ingredients in a pill. When they announce it, the country goes crazy because everybody knows we need more effective leaders. When they release it, it outsells Viagra.

The founders of the company start selling off stock and they call them Pillionaires. But along comes this guy who calls himself "the effective manager," and he challenges them to a no-pill challenge. If they identify two non-performing groups, he'll take on one and let somebody on the pill take another one, and he guarantees he will out-perform that person by the end of the year. They agree, but of course they give him a drug test every week to make sure he's not sneaking pills on the side.

I wrote the book with Marc Muchnick, who is a young guy in his early thirties. We did a major study of what this interesting "Y" generation—the young people of today—want from leaders, and this is a secret blend that this effective manager uses. When you think about it, David, it is really powerful on terms of what people want from a leader.

Number one, they want integrity. A lot of people have talked about that in the past, but these young people will walk if they see people say one thing and do another. A lot of us walk to the bathroom and out into the halls to talk about it. But these people will quit. They don't want somebody to say something and not do it.

The second thing they want is a partnership relationship. They hate superior/subordinate. I mean, what awful terms those are. You know, the "head" of the department and the hired "hands"—you don't even give them a head. "What do you do? I'm in supervision. I see things a lot clearer than these stupid idiots." They want to be treated as partners, if they can get a financial partnership, great. If they can't, they really want a minimum of psychological partnership where they can bring their brains to work and make decisions.

Then finally, they want affirmation. They not only want to be caught doing things right, but they want to be affirmed for who they are. They want to be known as individual people, not as numbers.

So those are the three ingredients that this effective manager uses. They are wonderful values when you think about them.

Rank-order values for any organization is number one, integrity. In our company we call it ethics. It is our number one value. The number two value is partnership. In our company we call it relationships. Number three is affirmation—being affirmed as a human being. I think that ties into relationships, too. They are wonderful values that can drive behavior in a great way.

Wright

I believe most people in today's business culture would agree that success in business has everything to do with successful leadership. In *The Leadership Pill*, you present a simple but profound premise, that leadership is not something you do to people, it's something you do *with* them. At face value, that seems incredibly obvious. But you must have found in your research and observations that leaders in today's culture do not get this. Would you speak to that issue?

Blanchard

Yes. I think what often happens in this is the human ego. There are too many leaders out there who are self-serving. They're not leaders who have service in mind. They think the sheep are there for the benefit of the shepherd. All the power, money, fame, and recognition moves up the hierarchy. They forget that the real action in business is not up the hierarchy—it's in the one-to-one, moment-to-moment interactions that your frontline people have with your customers. It's how the phone is answered. It's how problems are dealt with and those kinds of things. If you don't think that you're doing leadership *with* them—rather, you're doing it to them—after a while they won't take care of your customers.

I was at a store once (not Nordstrom's, where I normally would go) and I thought of something I had to share with my wife, Margie. I asked the guy behind the counter in Men's Wear, "May I use your phone?"

He said, "No!"

"You're kidding me," I said. "I can always use the phone at Nordstrom's."

"Look, buddy," he said, "they won't let *me* use the phone here. Why should I let you use the phone?"

That is an example of leadership that's done *to* employees not *with* them. People want a partnership. People want to be involved in a way that really makes a difference.

Wright

Dr. Blanchard, the time has flown by and there are so many more questions I'd like to ask you. In closing, would you mind sharing with our readers some thoughts on success? If you were mentoring a small group of men and women, and one of their central goals was to become successful, what kind of advice would you give them?

Blanchard

Well, I would first of all say, "What are you focused on?" If you are focused on success as being, as I said earlier, accumulation of money, recognition, power, or status, I think you've got the wrong target. What you need to really be focused on is how you can be generous in the use of your time and your talent and your treasure and touch. How can you serve people rather than be served? How can you develop caring, loving relationships with people? My sense is if you will focus on those things, success in the traditional sense will come to you. But if you go out and say, "Man, I'm going to make a fortune, and I'm going to do this," and have that kind of attitude, you might get some of those numbers. I think you become an adult, however, when you realize you are here to give rather than to get. You're here to serve not to be served. I would just say to people, "Life is such a very special occasion. Don't miss it by aiming at a target that bypasses other people, because we're really here to serve each other."

Wright

Well, what an enlightening conversation, Dr. Blanchard. I really want you to know how much I appreciate all the time you've taken with me for this interview. I know that our readers will learn from this, and I really appreciate your being with us today.

Blanchard

Well, thank you so much, David. I really enjoyed my time with you. You've asked some great questions that made me think, and I hope my answers are helpful to other people because as I say, life is a special occasion.

Wright

Today we have been talking with Dr. Ken Blanchard. He is coauthor of the phenomenal best selling book, *The One Minute Manager*. The fact that he's the Chief Spiritual Officer of his company should make us all think about how we are leading our companies and leading our families and leading anything, whether it is in church or civic organizations. I know I will.

Thank you so much, Dr. Blanchard, for being with us today.

Blanchard

Good to be with you, David.

About The Author

Few people have created more of a positive impact on the day-to-day management of people and companies than Dr. Kenneth Blanchard, who is known around the world simply as "Ken."

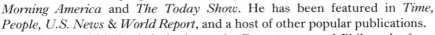

When Ken speaks, he speaks from the heart with warmth and humor. His unique gift is to speak to an audience and communicate with each individual as if they were alone and talking one-on-one. He is a polished storyteller with a knack for making the seemingly complex easy to understand.

Ken has been a guest on a number of national television programs, including *Good Morning America* and *The Today Show*. He has been featured in *Time, People, U.S. News & World Report*, and a host of other popular publications.

He earned his bachelor's degree in Government and Philosophy from Cornell University, his master's degree in Sociology and Counseling from Colgate University, and his PhD in Educational Administration and Leadership from Cornell University.

Dr. Ken Blanchard
The Ken Blanchard Companies
125 State Place
Escondido, California 92029
800.728.6000
760.489.8407
www.kenblanchard.com

Chapter Eight

An interview with...

Jim Dillahunty

David Wright (Wright)

Today we're talking with Dr. Jim Dillahunty. He has thirty years of experience as a highly successful CEO, entrepreneur, sales trainer, and public speaker. Dr. Dillahunty brings his thirty years of front-line experience together with his academic credentials in the field of organizational leadership to audiences around the world in keynotes, workshops, and through consulting. This unique combination of intense leadership experience and academic rigor makes Dr. Dillahunty uniquely qualified to bridge the gap between knowing and doing, and to present definitive

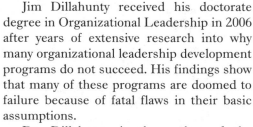
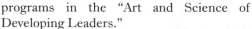

programs in the "Art and Science of Developing Leaders."

Jim Dillahunty received his doctorate degree in Organizational Leadership in 2006 after years of extensive research into why many organizational leadership development programs do not succeed. His findings show that many of these programs are doomed to failure because of fatal flaws in their basic assumptions.

Dr. Dillahunty is the author of the executive development series: *Fatal Flaws: What's Wrong With Our Leadership Development, and How to Fix It* (release date June 2008). The foremost *flaw* is that copying others makes us better leaders.

Jim has served for over ten years as a member of the Board of Directors of Responsibility, a non-profit organization that provides educational opportunities for Mexico's poorest citizens who live in the city's trash dump in Tijuana, Mexico. Jim serves on the Board of Directors of the San Diego Chapter of the U.S. National Speakers Association (NSA) and is a member of the International Federation of Professional Speakers (IFFPS), and the American Society for Training and Development (ASTD).

Dr. Dillahunty, welcome to *Blueprint for Success!*

Dr. Jim Dillahunty (Dillahunty)

Thank you, David!

Wright

Dr. Dillahunty, let's begin with how leadership should be defined.

Dillahunty

There are many, many definitions of the term "leadership," and over 16,000 book titles on the subject. Leadership is also one of the most popular topics for professional speakers. The working definition I developed in my academic research is: *Leadership is the initiative of individuals to utilize their knowledge, capabilities, power, and skills to marshal the forces of themselves and others toward some intended result, and in so doing leaders differentiate themselves from others by their influences and actions.* The key points in this definition are that leadership is *skills based* and requires *action.*

Wright

Our first question is one of the most frequently recurring questions in leadership development: how much of leadership skill comes along in our genetic make-up, and how much from our environment? Dr. Dillahunty, what does your experience say?

Dillahunty

The latest information I have from researchers at the University of Southern California suggests the attribution ratio is about seventy/thirty—70 percent of our leadership success comes from our environment, experiences and training, and 30 percent from our genetic inheritance and the circumstances of our birth.

Recently I conducted leadership workshops in the Republic of South Africa and Dubai. In Dubai the question of leadership as a birthright verses leadership through experience and training was an enthusiastic point of discussion. The succession of leaders in the United Arab Emirates, (UAE) from the founding father, Sheikh Zayed bin Sultan al-Nahayan, to the present ruler of Dubai, HH Sheikh Mohammed Bin Rashid Al-Maktoum, all were born into their positions of leadership. They have, however, proven themselves to be extraordinarily competent executives who leveraged the golden opportunities of their birthrights through education and experiences gained from fraternal mentoring.

In the Republic of South Africa (RSA) the most intense discussions centered on questions related to leadership development across a multitude of cultures. RSA has particular issues integrating the black and white citizens to overcome ethnic, linguistic, and cultural differences to achieve an enduring national identity.

Nelson Mandela, the first black President of the RSA, set an exceptionally high standard of leadership for the nation. His optimism and influence have encouraged a new generation of politicians, business leaders, and citizens to set aside past differences to develop new cadres of leaders. My assessment is that the experiences gained through the processes of mentoring in conjunction with education and training have the highest potential for leadership development in the RSA.

I am also asked the question: "Can leadership be taught?" The answer is, "No, leadership cannot be taught." It can however be *learned* and *self-taught* through our experiences and education. If leadership was simply a matter of education and instruction, our best business and political leaders would always come from academia. For individuals seeking to be better leaders— leaders who want to mentor others—success lies along the paths of *self-learning and experience not* by how many classes they have attended on the subject.

Related to the question of, "Can leadership be taught?" is "How much of success is determined by our genetic *nature*, verses our *nurturing* by experience?" and "How much does one's intelligence quotient (IQ) contribute to leadership success?" From my research and experience, IQ matters somewhat, but it is not a deciding factor. In business, if your IQ is too high it can be a liability because you communicate at a level that may be difficult and frustrating for others to follow. In scientific leadership, a high IQ is an asset—not so in business.

If you are born smart, or into a well-educated and prosperous family of influence—you have a significant head start, Life is easier if you are rich, smart, beautiful, and born to the right circumstances. The primary determinates of our success as business leaders, as family leaders, and the leadership skills we bring to our own lives are, however, not based on what we have been given, but on what we *do* with the skills we develop and what we *do* with the opportunities presented to us.

Wright

You're one of the few experts in the field of leadership development who have credentials from the trenches of experience as a CEO of a highly successful firm, as well as from your academic research. What are your observations about the state of leadership development today?

Dillahunty

I think there is a worldwide leadership crisis brewing; it's just over the horizon and will arrive in full force in less than ten years. There are three primary origins of this impending crisis: The first component is the continuous stream of scandals that emanate around the globe from the most senior corporate positions. These scandals undermine the public's *perceptions* of what leadership is and what leaders do. I use the term "perceptions" because in the minds of our customers, suppliers, and stakeholders, perceptions have equal validity with reality.

The second element driving the worldwide leadership crisis comes from the population shifts occurring in the developed economies and the Third World. These inexorable shifts in population demographics place entire societies at risk of not having a sufficient reservoir of leaders and leader trainers.

In the United States our population of experienced leaders is concentrated in the "Baby Boom" generation (born between 1945 and 1965). All these experienced leaders will retire en masse between 2010 and 2030. When these senior executives leave, they take their knowledge, their accumulated skills, courage, critical thinking, tenacity, and their insights with them, leaving the near $15 trillion U.S. economy in the hands of inexperienced and unseasoned managers. The Gen-Xers now in leadership training will have really big shoes to fill.

In other economies, both developed and emerging, are population bubbles that will affect national economic leadership. The population demographics in much of South America consist of young people coming into leadership positions without the benefit of mentors. Emergent leaders are left to fend for themselves without the guiding influences of mentoring leaders. Readers can find visual representations of the impending population shifts for most nations at http://www.census.gov/ipc/www/idb/.

The third element pushing this crisis to an imminent climax is the nature of business in the twenty-first century. Business firms of today can best be thought of as complex systems nested within equally complex subsystems. Isolated operations are no longer an option today. Much of this connectedness and interdependency is due to the Internet, which links *just about everything to just about everything else.* This arena of global connectivity and complexity has been the playground of Gen X and Gen Y, so they should feel right at home.

Three elements: scandals, population shifts, and systems complexity, are working together to create a worldwide leadership crisis that will mature within the next ten years.

Every leader knows from experience that within every crisis opportunities are present. In these times, for men and women who develop the right skills to find advantageous situations in times of chaos, the next decade represents *"the best of times and the worst of times"* for leadership advancement. If you have your leadership skills in order, your upward acceleration will leave you breathless.

Unfortunately, some organizations will wait until the crisis breaks upon them before reacting. Reacting to a crisis is for many, easier than solving a problem before it occurs.

Wright

It often fascinates me how our older and wiser people appear to be kicked out of leadership positions in some Western societies. Are they kicked out or are they just walking out?

Dillahunty

It is, I think, a little of both. Some senior executives are booted out for poor performance in a single quarter, and some to make room for the ascension of others. Many executives I work with, however, are fifty or sixty years of age and want more from their time on earth than ten- to fourteen-hour days in the corporate mill. They pack up their desks and leave to pursue latent and often philanthropic interests in their communities, or to follow an entrepreneurial siren.

In either case, senior executive departures can be traumatic, especially if they have not instituted programs of leadership training and succession. If they do not have the systems in place to properly develop the next cadre of leaders, the companies they leave often falter.

Wright

What do you see as the largest challenge that leaders face in the twenty-first century environment?

Dillahunty

There are many challenges unique to this new millennium. One that I think cripples long-term survival is the constant pressure on senior executives to focus on short-term results at the expense of long-term prosperity. In leadership terms, that means not taking time to develop your managers into leaders. It is the quality of the leaders in development who hold the keys to long-term success of the enterprise. Unfortunately, too many executives are seduced by the rewards of achieving short-term results at the expense of long-term survivability.

Another fatal flaw in leadership development that needs to be addressed is the belief by some that life is a *"zero sum game"*—all benefits in one area of life come at the expense of others; whatever we give to our leadership success in business is taken from our success in our family life or from our personal aspirations.

My research and my experience as an entrepreneur and CEO clearly highlight that the *skills of leadership* are really the *life skills* that we all seek. The most successful leaders I've interviewed and worked with are able to apply a consistent set of guiding skills in business, family, and personal settings. No doubt some of the success has been due to the collapse of the formal boundaries between business, family, and personal life. Today's executives are just as apt to leave work early to attend a child's ball game as they are to take work home. And few executives ever go on vacation without their cell phone and laptop at the ready!

Wright

You mentioned that there are *fatal flaws* in many leadership development programs. What are they and how do they interfere with our development efforts?

Dillahunty

Perhaps the most significant fatal flaw I encounter in leadership development programs is the assumption that we can acquire the attributes or skills of leadership simply by copying the behavior of other leaders. We mistakenly think that all we have to do to advance our leadership skills and potential for success in life is to find the best and brightest among us and *"do whatever they do"* and we will certainly *"have everything they have."* If we eat the same breakfast cereal, wear the same clothes, if we do all the things Warren Buffet and Bill Gates and other singularly significant individuals do, then surely we will have their success too. This is a pervasive false premise. Copying the behavior and traits of others does not bring us their skills or their successes!

Clay Christensen, author of *The Innovator's Dilemma*, used an analogy in one of his Harvard lectures to describe the origins of erroneously linking cause and effect. Our earliest ancestors observed magnificent eagles flying effortlessly in the sky above them and became envious. Being envious and inventive we took notes. According to our observations every bird has certain traits—certain characteristics—and if we could only copy them, we too could fly. So we proceeded to copy the birds and carefully build wings of feathers and fasten them to our backs.

We inadvertently made the false assumption that feathers and wings were the cause of flight in the same way we today make the false assumption that all we have to do to ensure our success in life is to copy the traits and behaviors of others. The point is: Copying the characteristics of birds does not make us capable of flight! Copying the characteristics of leaders does not make us capable of leadership!

This pervasive false belief—that copying the behavior and traits of successful people will guarantee *our* success—is the biggest single flaw in leadership development and personal development programs. Leadership is an emergent phenomenon, it comes from within, and it is not something that we can achieve by copying others. We can certainly learn from others, but copying only makes clones that look great on the surface, but lack the internal substance of leaders.

Wright

If we can't copy our way into successful positions of leadership, what is the path for aspiring managers to ascend to the ranks of CEOs, or for that matter parents who want to develop leadership skills in their children?

Dillahunty

Our leadership successes in business, in our families and for our self-actualizations are based squarely on a system of skills or guidance systems I call *"paradigm skill sets."* A paradigm is nothing more than templates—*mental guidance systems*—that direct all of our conscious behavior. As shown in the illustration, our paradigm skill sets are our central controllers and reside at the core of our beliefs, biases, perceptions, thoughts, cultures, and actions. So if we develop the right paradigms, we will have the requisite skills for advancement into the top executive ranks. The five paradigms I have identified can be learned and mastered at any age. Best of all, the paradigms are internalized uniquely within each individual and do not require us to copy the behaviors of others.

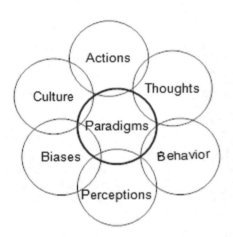

**Paradigms integrate all of the Systems
that define how we are in the world.**

Wright

If successful leadership development is a system, what are the components of that system?

Dillahunty

The five paradigms I have identified as critical components for success are 1) Social Capital, 2) Buoyancy, 3) Kaizen, 4) Facts & Values, and 5) Engagement.

Five is not a magic number; I group the skills as five paradigms because it represents a logical grouping(s). One could argue for seven or nine or more critical skill sets, but *five* was the logical grouping in my research and experience. A brief discussion of each of the five paradigms is as follows:

Social Capital is the network of relationships (both personal and professional) we build over our lifetime. In business *"who we know"* and more importantly *"who knows us"* have proved to be critical determinates in leadership success. When opportunities arrive, people think of you.

The benefits of Social Capital were clearly responsible for the rapid rise of General Eisenhower from the rank of U.S. Army Lieutenant Colonel in 1937 to Five-Star General in charge of all allied armies in Europe by 1942. His meteoric rise occurred because the *right* people knew him. When opportunity presented itself, Eisenhower's name came up in the discussions of promotable officers because his skills were known by senior staff. Many of today's executives credit their selection for top-level promotions to being a "known player." Social Capital should not be confused with being "the life of the party." Social Capital does not increase in proportion to the number of corporate functions we attend. Social Capital results from conscientiously developing key relationships and maintaining them through the arts of communication.

The second paradigm that successful leaders need to cultivate is, "Buoyancy." Buoyancy represents our ability to bounce back from adverse situations and experiences. Every human on the planet faces adversity. Life is a series on unpredictable events that we either capitalize on or they will destroy our self-confidence and willingness to act and take risks. There is a Japanese proverb that describes the Buoyancy we need for success in all life's endeavors: *"Fall down seven times, get up eight."* Every aspiring executive fails. Leadership and failure go together—if you are not failing you are not leading—failure goes with the territory of leadership. When we fail and bounce back, we have to bounce back wiser—we have to have learned valuable lessons from our missteps. We must bounce back smarter, with new facts, new insights, and new skills.

The third paradigm is *Kaizen* (continuous improvement). The term originates from the Japanese industrial practice of continually improving processes. I use it to mean that as executives we need to continually interact with our environment to improve ourselves and our ways of thinking. Just like the computer that sits on our desks, if we don't up-grade our hardware and our software every couple of years, they're functionally illiterate and obsolete.

There are two subsets to Kaizen processes that make continual learning much more effective: *time management and self-management.* Busy executives and productive people have systems that manage their time and a system for self-management. Together these two skills define the most industrious people. These paradigms contribute to our ability to continuously improve because we *do* have time to read the books, we *do* have time to go to the seminar, we *do* have time to go to yoga class, or just to sit and *think*.

The fourth paradigm represents the skills needed to integrate "Facts & Values" into decision-making. *Facts* represent the requisite quantitative and analytical skills needed by leaders to be effective in today's complex environment. *Facts* in themselves, however, do not contain any hint of value. And *Values* without facts are unsubstantiated beliefs and superstitions. Facts & Values need to be integrated within our ability to make judgments under conditions of stress and uncertainty.

Many of the scandals we have seen in the executive suites of our largest U.S. corporations have resulted from a singular concentration on monetary facts. The failures of firms like Enron, WorldCom, Adelphia, and others occurred when the facts & values of the organizations, their leaders, and the stakeholders were not compatible, and monetary *facts (we can make more money!)* won over corporate *values (we should do what is right!)*.

Leaders in manufacturing organizations face some of the toughest day-to-day challenges integrating Facts & Values into decision-making. Recently we have seen a spate of scandals coming from new Asian manufacturers who engage in the practice of "Quality Fading" (QF). QF means a manufacturer in a competitive environment submits bids with exceptionally low margins to win a contract. Once the contract is won, cheaper and inferior components and ingredients are substituted in order to raise the profit margins. QF represents a short-term financial victory (fact: *make more money*), at the expense of long-term survival (value: *take care of the customer*). On my Web site, www.NewParadigms.com, I propose rhetorical questions for executive readers that represent real case conundrums of integrating Facts & Values.

The fifth paradigm that binds all the skill sets is called "Engagement." It is the *doing*. If we have developed the paradigm skill sets: Social Capital, Buoyancy, Kaizen, Facts & Values, we need to deploy them consistently across the plane of our opportunities and experiences in life. If you have mastered all the other paradigms, but don't engage by *doing,* you risk becoming a skeptic. Many brilliant skeptics reside quite contentedly in bureaucracies and never actually initiate or do anything worthwhile. *Engagement is the tempering process of our experiences that turns ordinary iron into steel.*

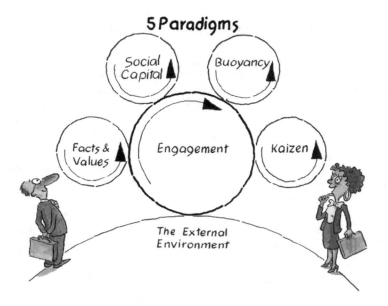

Wright

Do all the components of your system's approach have equal importance?

Dillahunty

To use Orwell's phraseology: *"All the paradigms are equal, but some are more equal than others."* The five paradigms, or guidance systems, are interactive, reactive, and can facilitate reactions. The five paradigms can serve as reagents in processes and as catalysts causing other elements to react. Just like catalytic reactions, the end result may have no resemblance to the ingredients, and may present no discernable trace of the catalyst itself.

I use the analogy of baking bread in my workshops. There are certain vital components—flour, water, leavening, salt, and heat. Like the five paradigms we have been discussing, the ingredients of bread are both reactive and interactive. Without any one of these components we are not going to produce the intended result.

I mentioned earlier that Engagement is the one skill set that binds all the paradigms together, so in response to your question *Engagement* is the pivot point for paradigms of equal value. We need to *engage* the skills we have learned. Engagement refines our paradigm skills through the heat of experience.

Wright

Is the system of paradigms the same for men and women executives?

Dillahunty

Yes, the five paradigms are universal and equally valid for men and women. But, since women are relatively new participants on the executive tracks, I believe there is an opportunity for them to significantly enhance their upward potential by developing Social Capital. Men have had the *old boy* network for a long time and women should likewise develop and benefit from their own proprietary networks of influence.

In the next few decades many more women will ascend into key executive positions because they are strategically positioned for advancement; 50 percent of our accountancy, law, and medical school students are women. Women executives may have a slight advantage over men due to their experiences with organizing the household and mentoring children that requires listening skills, self-discipline, and time-management skills, which are important parts of Kaizen principles.

Wright

From most of the books I've read on the subject, women are also better at relationships. Would that be part of Social Capital?

Dillahunty

From my experience and research I think women can be better at business relationships and team building because they seem to be adept at listening to others and assessing the non-verbalized feelings of others. These skills are part of our emotional intelligence (EQ) that has been popularized by Daniel Goleman and others.

Social Capital, to be of value for both men and women, must become a conscious effort. As upwardly mobile executives we need to examine our social and business relationships and determine if they are supportive of our interests. We need not be Machiavellian in the sense of only associating with those who can do us favors; rather, we need to conscientiously initiate and develop associations with supportive colleagues and family. When opportunities occur, often unpredictably from the kindest and cruelest turns of fate, the people of influence need to have you in the forefront of their thinking.

Wright

If an individual wants to develop leadership potential for themselves or if an organization wants to set up a leadership development program with a better than average chance of success, where is the starting point?

Dillahunty

Engagement is the key paradigm. When you start a project, you do not have to achieve 100 percent certainty of the path and the outcome before you start; you learn, correct, and adapt as you gain experience; but Engagement is the key.

If you are a "C" level leader (CEO, CFO, etc.), the best place to start is with your Human Resources department (HR). Once you get "buy-in" of the HR staff, they can set up the structure of a mentoring program using the five paradigms: Social Capital, Buoyancy, Kaizen, Facts & Values, and Engagement. The advantages of formal mentoring programs are: accountability, periodic reviews, and problem solving within the directed Engagement.

Wright

When you were discussing the five paradigms for successful leaders and indicated *"doing"* as a definition of Engagement, the first thought I had is that all the other paradigms might be irrelevant if you don't *do* something with them.

Dillahunty

You are correct in your observation. There is an apropos parable about three frogs sitting on a lily pad. One of them decides to jump off. How many frogs are left?

Wright

Probably three.

Dillahunty

That's right! You've got it, David. Because *deciding* to do something is not the same as actually *doing* it! So many of the objectives that executives develop in weekend leadership programs are only statements of intentionality. The mantras *"Yes, you can," "I've got the vision,"* and the popular slogan, *"Just do it,"* are meaningless without execution. Thomas Edison reminds us, *"There is no shortage of good ideas, only the horsepower to develop those that hold the most promise."*

Wright

Firms and executives have a lot on their organizational plates today. What are the benefits of successful leadership development programs? And can they be objectively measured?

Dillahunty

One of the major problems I see in leadership development programs today is that their results are never properly measured. There are many short-term conferences and executive retreats purporting to develop leaders and leadership skills. Attendees get all pumped up with "can-do" attitudes, platitudes, and T-shirts. But few executives ever review the development programs and ask the hard questions such as: "We spent a million dollars in our leadership development program last year. Where are the economic benefits?"

From my experiences there are two assessments that show whether or not leadership development programs are effective. The first is a qualitative assessment of the number of independent actions your employees initiate to support the goals and intentions of the organization's leaders. If the development program was a success, the intentions of the organization's leaders, as presented throughout the program, will be supported through the independent actions of others. Independent actions of managers and subordinates are the first noticeable changes that result from successful leadership development programs.

The second measure of leadership development success is quantitative. A recent international study involving five thousand senior executives from over forty countries placed a quantitative value on the outcomes of effective leadership development programs. Their data suggested that if your firm gets your leadership development done right, the benefits are on the order of a 20 percent marginal benefit "across the board"—productivity, profitability, and key employee retention.

Other studies indicated that if you *don't* get your leadership development programs done right, and you ignore the consequences of this leadership crisis; you face on the order of a 70 percent decline in productivity due to your key employees leaving. The employees who are left won't take independent action to support you, they wait until they're told to do something.

Wright

Dr. Warren Bennis, the author of numerous books on leadership, talks of the importance of vision in leadership. How do vision and intentionality fit within your new paradigms?

Dillahunty

On the subject of "leaders and vision," my experience would reinforce much of the thinking of Warren Bennis. Vision and intentionality however, are important, but only as long as they are drawn from a *basis in skills*.

For example, if I go out onto the golf course at Pebble Beach (I'm a non-golfer), and I have a perfectly clear vision and rock solid intention of hitting a magnificent 350-yard drive straight down the fairway, will it matter? If I close my eyes and clearly envision the ball in perfect alignment with the face of the club, and whisper to myself, "I can do it," over and over, louder and louder, do you think it would matter? No, it does not—not in the slightest. Why? Because all of my intentions, my crystal clear visions, and my mystical incantations are outside of my paradigm skill sets.

Now if Tiger Woods goes onto the course, and he clearly envisions a 350-yard drive straight down the fairway with single-minded intentionality, it really matters! Why does it matter for Tiger and not for me? Tiger Woods' vision and intentions are centered *within* his paradigm skill sets. Visions and intentions, without the dedication needed to develop the requisite skills, are irrelevant.

Wright

I have interviewed and worked with a great number of business leaders, and I subscribe to your "Engagement" proposition. Most of the people I see who are not successful or their self-image is low, don't engage. Who was it that said, "98 percent of failure comes from quitting"? And quitting is not doing, so I think your system of five paradigms is a really, really good system for leadership development.

About the Author

DR. DILLAHUNTY HAS THIRTY years of experience as a highly successful CEO, Entrepreneur, Sales Trainer, and Public Speaker. Dr. Dillahunty brings his three decades of front-line executive experience together with his academic credentials in the field of Organizational Leadership to audiences around the world in Keynotes, Workshops, Training, Teleconferences, Podcasts, and Consulting. This unique combination of intense leadership experience and academic rigor makes Dr. Dillahunty uniquely qualified to bridge the gap between knowing and doing.

Jim received his Doctorate degree in Organizational Leadership in 2006 and has observed from his academic research and experiences as a CEO that many leadership development programs are destined to fail because of fatal flaws in their basic assumptions. Dr. Dillahunty's programs are designed to inform, train, direct and motivate participants and organizations toward achieving their highest leadership potential.

Jim is also a member of the Board of Directors of Responsibility, a non-profit organization that provides educational opportunities for Mexico's poorest citizens who live in the city trash dump in Tijuana, Mexico. Jim serves on the Board of Directors of the San Diego Chapter of the U.S. National Speakers Association (NSA) and is a member of the International Federation of Professional Speakers (IFFPS) and the American Society of Training and Development (ASTD).

President Emeritus: *Fixed Income Securities, LP.*
7220 Trade St, Suite 310
San Diego, CA 92121   USA
www.NewParadigms.com
jdillahunty@msn.com
(O) 858-547-7750
(C) 858-220-4107 (US and Int'l)

Chapter Nine

An interview with...

Dr. Jeff Hockings

David Wright (Wright)

Today we are talking to Dr. Jeff Hockings. He was born and raised just outside of Niagara Falls, Canada. He graduated Chiropractic College in 1990 and proceeded to build and sell three practices for multi-millions during his first eleven years of business. He currently owns six different businesses with four of them producing passive income. He also owns his own commercial building as well as three residential homes and is currently building his custom dream home.

Dr. Hockings has invested over $400,000 during the past seventeen years to be mentored and trained by the best business minds in the country and has vigorously applied what he has learned.

He has been happily married to his wife, Traci, for fifteen years and they have a beautiful twelve-year-old daughter, Tiffani.

Dr. Hockings welcome to *Blueprint for Success.*

Dr. Jeff Hockings (Hockings)

Thanks, glad to be here.

Wright

What is your definition of success?

Hockings

My definition of success is having enough wealth and income to do what you want to do, when you want to do it, where you want to do it, for as long as you want to do it, not being dependent on anybody, not having any debt, living the dream, being able to do what you want every single day with your family, and giving to charities. That is my definition of success.

109

Too many people just don't have that. They are under someone else's thumb, they have so much debt and so much obligation they have to fulfill every day that it puts a lot of pressure on them and they are not free. That is what my ultimate goal of success is.

Wright

Independent wealth?

Hockings

Yes.

Wright

Why is goal setting over-rated regarding success?

Hockings

You hear a lot of things about goal-setting and it's not bad inherently, but the problem is that many people write down a goal, for instance, on January first and say that they want to have made this much and have gone here and have done that by the end of the year. That is great but they forget one important aspect—they don't make a plan to actually achieve that goal and then act on it. Just the fact of writing a goal down isn't enough. That is why I think it is over-rated. It is not necessarily a bad thing, but you need to also put a plan into effect and then act on that with a *huge* amount of motion to actually achieve that goal, otherwise it is not going to happen. Just putting up your goal board and looking at it every day is great, but you still have to do something.

One of my mentors told me that action is a lot better than meditation as far as achieving your goals.

Wright

What is the number one success principle you use?

Hockings

It is a combination of two things:

- Getting trained by mentors who have actually been where you want to go. Look at what they are doing and what they have done because you don't have to reinvent the wheel in many cases.
- Once you've found out what they have done, then you act on it. You take massive action along the same path that they've taken. When you do that you are guaranteed to have the same level of success as

they have. You don't have to reinvent the wheel but you *must* take massive action toward your goal to get the success that you want.

Wright

What is the biggest mistake people make that stops this success?

Hockings

It goes along with the action step. A lot of people won't plan where they want to be. Then once they do have a plan they don't take action on it.

So many people I know have great ideas. They've been to seminars, they've got warehouses full of books and home study courses and all of these million dollar ideas, but none of them ever get implemented. It is the inability to implement and to take action on what they've learned that holds people back. They have all these great ideas but they don't put them into action. You have to implement what you've learned to be ultra successful.

The most successful people I know are phenomenal implementers. They just take action on what they learn. It doesn't mean that they are smarter than anybody else, —they just have that ability to implement and take action on what they've learned.

Wright

You endorse the "Mastermind Principle." First would you tell our readers what the Mastermind Principle is? Is the Mastermind Principle really that important to success?

Hockings

The Mastermind Principle is where you get together with three, four, or five other like-minded people—people who are entrepreneurial, who think big, and they think outside the box. You get together with them three or four times a year in a room all by yourselves and just bounce ideas off each other. You take turns relating what you're working on and then explaining where your roadblocks are, and asking for advice and suggestions on how to overcome them. Everybody gets a turn. This is an excellent environment where you are with people with whom you feel comfortable sharing some of your crazy dreams and ideas that you might not feel comfortable sharing with anybody else. That is what the Mastermind Principle is.

As far as being important, it is absolutely critical. The more you get into success and the more things you learn you start finding there are less and less people you can actually share your dreams and ideas with who aren't going to be negative, who won't tell you how it can't work, who won't tell you that you're crazy and it's another big scheme. You don't want to be around people like that. This Mastermind Group is very, very critical to your success. Again, most of the successful people I know have some form of Mastermind Group they meet with a minimum of once a year or even by phone and conference call a couple of times a year. This way they can share ideas with each other and brainstorm with each other. If there are four people in a room, a fifth brain is created and synergy happens with these like-minded people. The amount of progress you can make toward your goal and planning is just phenomenal in the Mastermind setting.

Wright

I imagine that you put a great emphasis on the people with whom you associate. Does it really matter?

Hockings

It is critical. Jim Rohn said that if you take the average income of the five people you associate with the most, your income would be the same or nearly the same as theirs. If you are hanging around people who are making $25,000 a year and are negative, whiners, and complainers that is pretty much where you are going to be. Sometimes it is necessary to eliminate some friendships as you start climbing the success ladder, otherwise they tend to bring you down to their level. You need to associate with people who have no poverty consciousness and no fear of success so that when you are with them you are motivated and inspired. If you are always trying to motivate and pull your friends up to your level it gets exhausting after a while. Sometimes you have to make some hard decisions and not spend as much time with the people in your life who are negative and who have that 9 to 5 job mentality. That might not be where you want to be.

Look at your friends. It is very, very critical who you associate with. You don't want to be around people who are consistently negative and putting you down or putting down some of the dreams, goals, and ambitions you have.

Wright

Mentors must be very important for success. How do you develop mentors?

Hockings

Mentors are critical. One of the master keys of my success in the last seventeen years since being out of school is that I look for different mentors and am trained by experts and top minds in business and marketing.

There are two different types of mentors. You can actually have "silent mentors"—mentors who don't even know you. You buy everything they have put out there, you go to all their seminars, read all their books, and then follow what they say. The other form of mentoring is hiring somebody as your personal one-on-one coach and that person becomes your mentor as well.

The purpose of mentoring is to find somebody who has the income that you want, has the lifestyle that you want, the free time with family, great health, and everything that you want. You go up to that person and say, "You seem to be where I want to be, would you be willing to let me hire you as my mentor—as my coach?'

That is as simple as it is. Most people who are very successful either already have a mentor or coaching program in place and you can hire them. If they don't and you go up and ask them, maybe you can work something out, even if it just involves going to their business and following them around for a few days. Just by seeing it actually being done by some of these successful people takes you to the next level as far as your ability to think bigger when you actually see it being done. Mentorship is a critical component. You've got to find people who are where you want to be and follow in their footsteps, and then you will have the same amount of success. It is just a proven principle.

Wright

How does taking risks affect your success?

Hockings

I think that if you really want to have a tremendous amount of success and wealth in life you've got to take some risks. That is just the way it is. There are calculated risks and there are risks where you look at all the down sides and look at what is the worst thing that can happen. Then you plan for that. It is more risky being too comfortable and staying inside your comfort zone. That is even more risky to your financial future.

A lot of people think that they don't want to leave their job because it is too risky to go out on their own. They think it's risky to start their own business. Yes, there are some risks, but so is being an employee. As an employee you have zero control over your financial future because the boss or the corporation could close down tomorrow without any warning and you're out on the street. That doesn't happen when you are the actual boss of your own life. You have full control that way.

A lot of people think they are being more conservative and planning for their future by staying in their job when in actuality the opposite is true. If you look at most successful people they are risk-takers to some degree. They will try things and fail and try another thing and fail but they keep stepping up to the plate and taking a swing.

Babe Ruth had the highest number of homeruns during his career but he also had the highest number of strikeouts. When he was up to the plate he swung for the fences every single time and it was either a homerun or it was a strikeout. Sometimes in business you have to do that as well. You've got to swing for the fences. Not everything is going to be a homerun but you'll have enough of them to have incredible success and wealth, even though many of your business ventures might fail. Just make sure that you look at the down side. What is the worst thing that could happen? Plan for that and you will have all the success and wealth you ever dreamed of.

Wright

How do you think personal health affects success?

Hockings

Number one, as a Doctor of Chiropractic, I have a bias toward this. I think you really need to be healthy to be successful. To run multiple businesses and be an entrepreneur and spend the hours and time necessary to build a great business you've got to have energy. You've got to have physical fitness otherwise you get exhausted by 3:00 or 4:00 in the afternoon. It doesn't look good when you are trying to make deals and you are seventy to eighty pounds overweight. Going into a business meeting looking like that doesn't portray the best image as far as confidence, professionalism, and vitality. This is different than when you are in shape, you feel strong, you are working out, you are standing taller, and you look proud and successful. That is all part of it. Health is very, very important to your success because you have to have that energy—not only mental but physical—so you can actually handle all the different business ventures you will be involved in when you become an entrepreneur and become more successful in your life.

Many wealthy people don't focus on their health enough and therefore develop major diseases. They can't even enjoy the wealth they have created. You need to have balance.

Wright

Down through the past few decades I've always heard to focus, focus, and focus—do one thing and get good at it. You have done the opposite of that in owning so many businesses. Is it a good idea to have multiple businesses?

Hockings

There are two answers to that one. Number one is that you don't want to ever try to get a second, third, or fourth business going if you can't make your first business successful. A lot of people will try—they'll have a failing business and want to start another one. Then they will have two failing businesses, which won't make it better. In my profession, a lot of Chiropractors will try to open up a second office thinking that they will double their income. Typically what happens is they have just doubled their overhead but they are making the same income as they did when they had only one office. It isn't really a smart business move.

You have got to make sure you are making a profit, that the business is up and running by reliable staff members, and that you don't actually have to be in the office. Then you are stable enough to start the next business and repeat the process.

That is why I think ultimately having multiple businesses is much better—you won't have all your eggs in one basket. That happens a lot; people focus all their energy on one thing and when that fails they have no back up plan. They have to start from scratch all over again. That is why the philosophy I have now is in multiple streams of income. I have six different businesses that are working and if one of those businesses fails I've got five others that are producing income for me. I don't have all my eggs in one basket.

My wife and I made a mistake about ten years ago. We had a little temporary crisis in our office due to an insurance billing problem. We literally almost lost the business. We had no plan B. I made a promise to her back then that we will never be dependent on just one source of income ever again. I have stuck to that promise and now we have six businesses and more in the hopper. We're just waiting to get all six of the ones we have now running on autopilot with properly trained staff and partners and then we will have time to go and start the next one. I think multiple businesses are the way to go as long as you set them up properly.

Wright

Are your businesses similar or are you talking about different businesses?

Hockings

Three of the six are in the Chiropractic field but the other three are totally unrelated. It is just a matter of looking at every business opportunity that comes your way and deciding if it is something that can make you a high amount of income while spending as little time as possible. That is the whole idea. If you are running six businesses you can't have all six of those requiring forty hours of your time per week. It's impossible. That is what you have to look at and that is what I look at now when I am analyzing a new business opportunity. How much time is it going to take me per week to do this and what is the potential return on a monthly basis by doing this? Is it worth it? If it is only going to make me a couple thousand a month I am not interested. If it makes me $15,000 to $20,000 extra per month then it has my attention.

Wright

How do you suggest that our readers and listeners establish long-term success?

Hockings

The best way that I've seen is to create the habit of saving. When you put a consistent amount of money away on a weekly or monthly basis in your wealth account—money you don't touch—then eventually after ten, fifteen, or twenty years there will be enough money there where you could actually be debt free. You will have enough money to live on the rest of your life even if you decide not to work any longer.

This doesn't mean you save and save until you are sixty-five or seventy and retire like we are trained to think. You put enough away so that you can retire early if you choose to. If you still want to work, you can, but you are working at things you want to do, they are totally under your control, on your timeline, you are working with people you want to work with, and you're not feeling that you have to work to pay your bills. That is the biggest long-term success strategy.

You experience freedom and success when you don't owe anybody anything. You have enough money set aside so that you don't have to work if you don't want to. That is where you really have true control over your long-term success—by continually saving. Start off with 2 percent of the money you make every week or month if you have to. Saving 10 percent or higher would be the ultimate goal. It is amazing—when you do that on a regular basis it creates momentum. It is amazing, after a year or two you will be surprised how much money is in your wealth account. It makes you feel great that the money is there. You are putting it away and you don't touch it. It is not for emergencies or anything else. That is your wealth retirement account. This is one of the biggest strategies that I've seen for really taking control of your long-term success in addition to having multiple businesses giving you passive income.

Wright

What is the one universal success strategy you endorse?

Hockings

It goes back to implementation and taking action. Most people reading this book or listening to this interview that we are doing have probably been to seminars or read books and have received many ideas on what they know they could do to be more successful, either starting their own business, having an Internet site, or whatever it is. It is not a lack of knowledge about what they should do, it's their inability to implement and take action on what they know they should do.

A great example of this is weight loss. Most people know they shouldn't eat chocolate and chips and drink cola every day. And they know they shouldn't lie around and watch television five hours every day. Most people know that this is not the way to health. They know what they should be doing and what they shouldn't be doing. The trick is having them take action on what they already know they should do. This is another instance where a mentor and/or a Mastermind Group—people who can hold you accountable—are important.

The one universal success strategy is implementing and taking action on what you already know you should be doing to be more successful. You can get all the mentoring and training you want and they could give you 1,000 great ideas, but if you don't take action on those ideas it's not going to happen. You can't have somebody else do your push-ups for you. You've got to get into the gym and do them yourself. It is the same thing with success and with business. You've got to actually do it. That is the biggest thing— there is no greater one than that. Most people have an abundance of ideas but they just don't implement and take action on them.

Wright

What a great conversation I really appreciate the time you've taken with me this morning to answer these serious questions. If people are looking for success I think you have a pretty good idea here.

Hockings

I appreciate it. It was my pleasure to be on the "call."

Wright

Today we've been talking with Dr. Jeff Hockings. He currently owns six different businesses with four of them producing passive income. He also owns his own commercial building as well as three residential homes and is currently building his custom dream home.

Over the past seventeen years he has invested over $400,000 to be mentored and trained by the best business and marketing minds in the country. He has vigorously applied what he has learned. No wonder he is successful.

Jeff, thank you so much for being with us today on *Blueprint for Success.*

About the Author

Dr. Jeff Hockings was born and raised just outside of Niagara Falls, Canada. He graduated Chiropractic College in 1990 and proceeded to build and sell three practices for multi millions during his first 11 years of business. He currently owns six different businesses with four of them producing passive income. He also owns his own commercial building as well as three residential homes. Dr. Hockings has invested over $400,000 during the past seventeen years to get mentored and trained by the best business minds in the country and has vigorously applied what he has learned. He has been happily married to his first wife, Traci, for fifteen years and they have a beautiful twelve-year-old daughter, Tiffani.

Dr. Jeff Hockings
79245 Corporate Center Drive, Suite 100
La Quinta, California 92253
888.608.8464
drjeffhockings@yahoo.com
www.DrJeffHockings.com

Chapter Ten

An interview with...

Jay Niblick

David Wright (Wright)

Today we are talking to Jay Niblick, researcher, entrepreneur, lecturer, and author. Jay is founder and Chief Executive Officer of Innermetrix Incorporated, an international consulting firm with offices in North America, the United Kingdom, France, South Africa, and Australia. He is a thought leader in the field of axiology, the science of decision-making created by Professor Hartman of Yale and MIT Universities. Jay has helped organizations on five continents understand the most important, yet least understood aspect of success—decision-making. He is author of the *Attribute Index Decision-Making Profile,* which has sold over 300,000 copies. His work on the Board of the Hartman Institute at the University of Tennessee has added to his expertise in understanding how the most successful people make decisions.

Jay, welcome to *Blueprint for Success.*

Jay Niblick (Niblick)

Thank you very much David, I appreciate the invite.

Wright

What is the topic of this chapter?

Niblick

This chapter is about what the results of significant research has revealed about how the most successful people think about success. More accurately, it is about how these successful people "think" to be successful.

Did you ever have that one class in school where no matter how hard you studied you always seemed to struggle? Regardless of the effort you put in, the grades never came easily. Did you also have another subject, however, where the exact opposite was true, where you just sailed through and "got it" with little to no effort? In each case, there was probably someone else in the class who was the opposite of you.

We've all experienced some example of this either in school or at work or in athletics. This is because individual cognitive talents are unique to everyone. This isn't just true of school, but basically all of life. Every one of us can name many abilities in which we are proficient and therefore enjoy doing (e.g., being creative, solving problems, socializing, etc.). We can all also name many abilities we don't have or in which we don't excel (e.g., being proactive, attention to detail, delegating, etc.).

A common problem of adulthood is that when we finish school and begin working, many of us assume that it is our responsibility to develop all the talents required by our jobs. Somehow, it is our responsibility to do everything well. On the rare occasion when our job's requirements are perfectly aligned with our own talents, this is fine. In most cases, however, this is not true and we find ourselves trying to utilize non-existent talents or develop weaknesses to be successful. Many people spend precious energy trying to "fix what is wrong with them" instead of focusing more on what they do well and learning how to succeed with their strengths.

The old belief about individual performance was a formula that indicated: intelligence + hard work = success. The old mantra was that if you are smart and you work hard enough, you can succeed at anything. How many times have you heard, "you can be anything you want to be"? This kind of thinking is great and inspirational, and while not entirely false, it is missing something. The problem with the old "be smart and work hard" equation is that it assumes all people are created equal. While a wonderful sentiment for the founding fathers and our legal rights, this simply is not true when it comes to our abilities. Yes, we all do have talents, and we all do have the same arguably infinite potential, but our talents are not all the same. When we tell people that they can be anything they want to be if they try hard enough, many of them—the large majority—spend their lives trying to develop their weaknesses so they can be great in the things they feel are important for success in a given role or career. This is not what our study found that the most successful people do.

Our talents exist for many varied and different purposes, and so too must the paths to our success be equally as unique and individual. The extremely successful people we studied understand this and instead of spending their time trying to become great doing things that are not a natural talent for them based on how they think and make decisions, they accept those limitations and choose instead to focus on leveraging the talents they do have. In other words, they are much more aware of what abilities they have and do not have than most people. They acknowledge their weaknesses more than most and instead of focusing on developing weaknesses as most do, they are more concerned with maximizing the talents they already have and minimizing dependence on their weaknesses.

Here's their secret: the most successful people have figured out that success comes faster and more completely when they learn to work from their strengths. It comes faster and more easily when they decide not to focus on what they do not do well, but choose instead to take what they already have and use it more effectively. Success comes when they focus on being true to themselves, not "fixing" themselves. These successful people have learned how to be *authentic* to what they do best, and then they discover where and what kind of work fits those talents best. They do not work backward as most people do—deciding what role or job they want and then trying to change themselves to fit that job. The successful people make their roles fit them, not the other way around.

The new formula for success may still be intelligence plus hard work, but the most successful among us add self-awareness and authenticity to that formula. The successes they achieve make a very compelling argument for listening to what they have to say.

Wright

How does it relate to the theme of this book, *Blueprint for Success?*

Niblick

At its core, our work focuses on individual success—what supports it, what hampers it, and how to measure and develop it. I would title this chapter "What's Your Genius?" because it concerns the lessons learned about what makes some people so successful—what makes successful people geniuses at what they do?

Our use of the term "genius," by the way, differs from the traditional use. It doesn't describe superior intellect or IQ. When we see people who have reached the top of their field, who are the best of the best at whatever they do, they are often considered pure geniuses at what they do. Among those we interviewed for this study were: a world-renowned personal excellence coach, the founder of a dot-com juggernaut, multi-million dollar management consultants, one of the top fifty executive coaches in the world, one of the best personal assistants in Hollywood, star athletes, perennial Forbes and *Wall Street Journal* interviewees, Fortune 100 CEOs, world-authority physicians, and several *New York Times* best-selling business and self-help authors. We considered as wide a scope of roles and specialties as we could to find correlations.

What we found was that geniuses could exist in any role. Yes, many of those we interviewed were famous, but we met genius auto mechanics and genius waiters, too. We have seen genius salespeople and genius support staff as well. Sure, some of those we studied may indeed be intellectual geniuses, but when we talk about *successful* geniuses we are talking about those who have figured out how to leverage their God-given natural talents into the best performance and ultimately the best successes in any role.

This book is about finding a blueprint for success. I can't think of a better fit for such a journey then the findings of research dedicated to just that—success. This chapter will review some startling findings on key ingredients to being successful. It will also provide some practical, easy-to-apply lessons that anyone can benefit from.

Wright

Will you summarize the findings of your research for our readers?

Niblick

Our company, Innermetrix, is a management-consulting firm. One of the ways we help our clients around the world is to help them understand and develop top performers. This work exposes us to a very diverse group of companies and top performers and it just seemed like an obvious fit to use those contacts to study what made the most successful people tick.

Seven years ago, we began conducting research designed to answer the following questions:

- Where do natural thinking and decision-making talents come from?
- How do they affect our professional and personal successes?
- Can they really be measured?
- Can they be leveraged to achieve greater success with less effort?

Having studied an enormous database of top performers from around the world containing tens of millions of pieces of information, we are now able to answer these questions. Based on these results, I'm in the process of writing an entire book on this subject titled *What's Your Genius? How The Best Think About Success.* Among the many things we learned was the importance of one of the most vital yet least understood aspects of success—decision-making. Unlike many other treatments on individual success that focus on behavior, personality, or intelligence, our findings paint a clear picture, perhaps for the first time, of how our subconscious decision-making processes directly affect our success.

Here is what we learned. There are indeed distinct and identifiable characteristics that are shared by the most successful people. If I had to summarize it in one statement, it would be: "those who are more aware of their natural talents and who are true to them achieve greater success with less effort."

Specifically, we found five distinct traits unique to the most successful among us. We call these the *Success Traits:*

- Self-awareness
  - o Self-concept
  - o Role awareness
  - o Self-belief
- Authenticity
- Unique Definition of Success

Success is about awareness and authenticity, and about being true to who you are, not wasting energy trying to become something you are not. The late Professor Robert Hartman, a brilliant researcher in the field of thinking and decision-making, once said, "Stop trying to put in what God left out, and instead, work with what He put in." I think the lessons we learned in our study would support this exactly. The most successful people say there are many skills they do not possess and many skills they do not do well. They simply don't depend on those skills for their success. This may sound like a no-brainer, "Gee, do what you do well to be successful. Thanks for that, Mr. Obvious." Unfortunately, the majority of people don't understand this concept! They lose site of their own unique talents and seek to possess new ones or become something they are not just to fit some role or job. It's so easy to do. Someone you admire at work tells you that you need to be a more strategic thinker or be more empathetic. Self-help books convince you that in order to succeed you must eliminate certain weaknesses and develop specific talents.

The fact is that this is simply not true and our work proves it. The most successful people don't share any common talents. What they do share in common is the level of awareness about whatever those talents are, and the degree of honesty they have with themselves in being true to those talents and not trying to change who they are.

These talents can be for anything, by the way. For some, it is their uncanny ability to see the flaw in any strategy or understand someone's emotions or fears. For others it is an ability to always see the big picture on the playing field or just intuitively diagnose the mystery illness. The key factor for all of these individuals is that they know what their strengths are and they ensure that their success is dependent on those strengths, not their weaknesses. If they are not great at strategic thinking, they admit it and make sure that their roles focus on the tactical aspects of accomplishing results. They rely on others to work on the more strategic aspects. If they are not gifted at being empathetic, they own up to it and make sure that possessing high levels of emotional intelligence is not a mandate for success in the goals they set. This makes these geniuses real people, just like you and I are. They have all the flaws and weaknesses the rest of us share. They make just as many mistakes as the next guy and as regular humans, they own up to this fact. The way in which they are different, however, is that I think they do a better job of listening to themselves and learning from what does and does not work for them. It is this authenticity that aligns everything they do with everything they do well. When this happens, they truly are a genius at what they do.

Based on these natural talents, everyone has the ability to be a genius. The most successful among us have somehow managed to figure this out when so many of us have not.

Perhaps a quote from one of the interviews sums it up best. As Dr. Marshall Goldsmith said, "There are a lot of things I stink at. I just do a very good job of making sure I don't have to do them to be successful."

Wright

Will you give us some specifics?

Niblick

Our research was conducted on over 24,000,000 bits of data gathered over a seven-year period on more than 300,000 people. We used a science created by Professor Robert S. Hartman at Yale and M.I.T universities that measures a person's thinking or decision-making style. A profile was administered to individuals online, and in 99 percent of the cases, a one-on-one interpretation was given to the individual to ensure accuracy and gather feedback. We compiled the data and used statistical analyses to determine what correlations existed among the top performers.

Top performers were determined by a variety of factors gathered by the debriefing consultants at the time of interpretation (e.g., performance in their roles, longevity, management and employee reviews, and personal satisfaction). To back up what the data showed, we also conducted over 10,000 personal interviews that involved a more in-depth interpretation to get an even more personal perspective on what the data were telling us.

One of the first and most interesting findings from the study was that there were no specific ways of thinking that were more prevalent among top performers than any other. As I said in the opening discussion, there was no single talent that was shared among all the top performers. What we did find, however, were correlations among the ways in which these successful people viewed those talents, how aware of them they were, and how true to them they were. Since there is no one "success talent," only successful ways to understand and use those talents, anyone can learn to be more successful. This means that it isn't about being born with certain special talents.

We found that the most successful people did share those five things in common that I just mentioned; what we call the five *Success Traits:* self-concept, role awareness, self-belief, authenticity, and a unique definition of success.

Wright

Will you talk a little bit more about each of the components of success that you identified? What are these *Success Traits*?

Niblick

The first three success traits fall under one main heading called "self-awareness." This is about knowing yourself, your talents, where you want them to take you, and how you will get there.

The first Success Trait is called *Self-Concept.* This is the vision you have for where you are going or how clearly you see what you want to become. It is your point B on your map in a way.

When people have a highly developed self-concept they have a great sense of certainty about where they are going. They are confident in their direction in life. This certainty and confidence help them overcome obstacles in their way and drive them onward toward their chosen objectives. When they have a clear self-concept, they understand what their natural talents are and have a clear picture in their head of where they want those talents to take them. I'm not talking about just a *good* idea of where I'm going. The most successful people have a *crystal clear* picture in their head of where they are going. They can smell, feel, and taste what it is like to actually stand in that place where they see themselves sometime in their future.

People with low levels of self-concept lack this confidence and certainty. They don't clearly see where they want to go. They are like a ship at sea without a course or final destination. They may be working very hard aboard that ship to make things run well, but in the end, all that work often doesn't get them anywhere specific because they don't have a final destination in the first place.

As a result of their lack of clarity for where they are going, these people often end up letting the present control where they go in the future. One significant side effect of low self-direction is what we call "shifting"—a person shifts focus very frequently from one direction to another. This continual shifting causes people to never fully commit, and usually leaves a lot of unrealized potential sitting on the table because without an end objective, they have nothing to apply those talents to.

The most successful people have lots of certainty and high scores in the self-concept dimension. They have very clear pictures in their head of where they see themselves going. They can describe it with such clarity that you can almost feel it yourself.

Wright

And role awareness?

Niblick

The second Success Trait under self-awareness is called *Role Awareness.* If self-concept is where I am going, role awareness is what I do today to get there. Since we talked about self-concept being the point B on your map, role awareness is the vehicle or actions you take to get to point B.

People who have role awareness clearly understand their roles in life. They have a very clear understanding of the meaning, value, goals, and objectives of their various roles in life and how they interact.

People with high levels of role awareness understand what they are doing today. Their roles connect with their self-concept in their understanding of what they must do today to reach their future self-concept. These people tend to be very comfortable with their different roles in life. They receive personal reward and gratification from them. They enjoy and connect themselves with their roles and are very confident in them.

People with low levels in this dimension suffer from what we call "role confusion." They do not clearly see what their roles are or they doubt them or want to change them somehow. As a result of this ambiguity they do not perform to their fullest potential because they simply are not sure *how* to perform.

The most successful people have very high levels of role awareness and are very clear about what their roles in life are and how they need to do them.

Wright

The third Success Trait is called *Self-belief.* How is that defined?

Niblick

Self-belief deals with the level of belief people have in themselves and their ability to succeed. This is the level of appreciation they have for themselves and their belief that they can indeed do what is needed to succeed. It is very dependent on the other two components of self-awareness because when you are certain of where you are going and confident in what you have to do to get there, your level of self-belief is higher. However, when you are uncertain about where you are going (low self-concept), and don't clearly understand how to get there (role confusion), your level of belief in your own ability to get there goes down as well.

People with high levels of self-belief have positive scripts they play over and over in their head. They truly believe in themselves and assume that they will succeed. They can develop a certain sense of self-entitlement: "of course I can do it; why wouldn't I?" They tend to weather storms better, survive hard times longer, and are not as prone to significant self-doubt.

People with low levels of self-belief suffer from self-limiting beliefs. They have lots of self-doubt that typically interferes with their ability to maximize their natural talents. They can become seekers of approval—seeking always to gauge their self-confidence based on the opinions of others. They can lack confidence, optimism and, in extreme cases, even become paralyzed with self-limiting beliefs and doubt. Very often, the result of low self-belief is seen in people who seek to recreate themselves as what they perceive more successful people are. They are the most prone to trying to change who they are into someone else. If you don't believe in something, it makes sense to try and swap it for something else. When you think about the theory of personal development that promotes fixing yourself, it requires the presupposition that you are broken in the first place.

The most successful people don't automatically assume they are broken to begin with. They have higher levels of self-belief than normal. My personal thoughts on the whole "attack your weaknesses" mentality is that if I am to assume I need so much fixing, I must first assume I am broken and to assume I am that broken is to assume God made a mistake. I'm not egotistical enough to think that I know more about how I should have been made. When I think about it like this, it helps me feel comfortable with accepting who I am and seeking not to change what I am, but how I apply what I am.

Wright

You mentioned two more Success Traits. Will you talk a little about them as well? What does "being authentic" mean?

Niblick

The fourth Success Trait we found to be common among the most successful people we studied was that they are *Authentic*. When we talk about being authentic, we mean that they are true to themselves. They don't try to fool themselves into thinking that they are something other than what they are. They admit their limitations and own up to them. While many people admit their limitations, where the most successful people differ is that they don't then try to change this fact. When each one of them, without fail, received their decision-making profile, they didn't hone in on the weaker areas and ask, "How do I fix that?" Instead, all of them focused on the highest scores and asked how they could leverage them to their best advantage. They started connecting their high scores (talents) to their successes in life and highlighting how they managed to avoid dependence on their weaknesses.

Is it a question of optimism versus pessimism? Marty Seligman, in his book, *Learned Optimism,* discusses the dramatic effects of optimism and pessimism on people's success and happiness in life. While I do think it does play a role—perhaps a significant one—I unfortunately can't say exactly how much because we haven't studied that aspect directly. I do think there is something to be said for the argument that successful people look at the positives of their profile, whereas many more unsuccessful people choose instead to focus on the negatives, so I definitely think there is a link.

Many people have been told that success is a matter of correcting what is wrong with them, and believe that in order to succeed they must first eliminate all weaknesses; the most successful among us don't share this opinion. They have somehow managed to either not get this message or they simply don't buy it.

Where this difference comes from we can't say. What we can say with certainty, however, is that this difference exists. Some tell us that they were taught very early in life by their parents that they should respect who they are and try to find activities and work that allow them to be true to their natural talents and drivers. Others tell us that they feel a sense of independence and have never been big on following the crowd or conforming to what others say they should or should not be.

Regardless of the reason, what we do know is that the most successful people don't buy into the common belief that they should spend countless hours and vast amounts of energy trying to develop all their weaknesses. They simply don't believe it is worth it, and their successes are hard to argue with.

Perhaps the most important thing isn't to understand what led to this commonly held belief among the most successful people, but instead just embrace the fact that it exists and learn from it. In the end it is the setting of goals and deciding on directions that offer us the greatest potential to become truly genius at whatever we do. I think we can all learn from these people just how important it is to be authentic.

Wright

The fifth and final trait is what?

Niblick

The final Success Trait we discovered, and the one that was also the biggest surprise, was what we call *a unique definition of success.* That definition was one of *happiness as success.*

Again and again we heard the successful people tell us how they don't think about success in the same way that most people do. We weren't trying to understand what their definition of success was at all, but even though we did not ask, each one of them shared the opinion that their definition of success was not the definition most people might have—monetary success or competitive success or things like fame, land, status, etc.

The successful people in our study all defined success as being truly happy with themselves and what they did. Some described success as never having a job, but a passion for something they love to do regardless of reward or pay. Most told us that finding one's passion *is* finding one's genius. Some talked about success as being fulfilled and feeling whole in their roles and life. Some talked about feeling successful because of their lengthy marriage or loving relationship with their children. Not one person said I am successful because I made so many millions, although many on the list have. None of them said they set out to succeed at taking more than others or having more or being worth more. Do not get me wrong. I am sure these geniuses enjoy money, security and fame as much as any other. I am simply saying that when they speak of how they define success, while they include these more common drivers, they place much more emphasis on those things not as commonly seen or expected.

In other words, the typical indicators of success were not the main drivers for the successful people we met. They all seemed to qualify their success much more by the degree of happiness and passion they achieved in the work they do.

Wright

If I understand you correctly, the five traits can be developed?

Niblick

Yes, these traits can be developed. The lessons learned in our research is that natural talents cannot easily be developed, but the learned traits we have for how we use those talents can very much be developed, and quickly.

We all have natural talents for how we think and make decisions, but these do not change much over the course of our lives. These are what I call "glacially dynamic," which simply means that they do change, but very slowly over the course of our lives. We all know that we don't think about things the same when we are forty as we did when we were sixteen. These talents do develop over the course of our lives, but they are not something that we can sit down and create over a weekend or even with months of dedicated work. What is dynamic, however, and what can be developed very quickly is our ability to understand these natural talents and apply them better. The five things we discovered by studying the most successful people (e.g., self-concept, role-awareness, self-belief, authenticity, and their definition of success) are all things that anyone can develop to become more successful.

If we can learn anything from these successful people, it is that we can all make dramatic improvements in how we see ourselves, how we appreciate ourselves, and how we apply ourselves.

Wright

Are there practical steps that anyone can take from these finding to become more successful?

Niblick

Here are just a few ways in which you can develop your success traits. These are things we have done with many people around the world and they are remarkably effective. We will look at six simple things you can do right now to develop your genius and become more successful:

Step Number 1—*What's Your Genius,* the Book: As I mentioned earlier, due to the amount of information we gathered on this topic, I'm writing an entire book about what we found and how anyone can benefit from this information. It will be called *What's Your Genius? How the Best Think About Success.* It should be out early 2008, so visit www.whatsyourgenius.com to find out more.

Step Number 2—Measuring Self-Awareness: We used a profile called the "Attribute Index" to actually measure the individual decision-making styles of those we worked with and studied. This profile is a very unique and powerful tool that measures natural talents based on thinking and decision-making styles, but it also measures the level of self-awareness. By being able to actually measure these elements, we were able to help people identify and understand their unique talents better. To find out how you can get your own Attribute Index profile and work on your own Success Traits, send an e-mail to questions@innermetrix.com.

Step Number 3—Developing a Strong Self-Concept: One of the ways in which we help our clients develop a clearer self-concept is called *Future*

Visioning. It is a process of creating a more realistic and detailed picture of where you want to go—in work or in life.

The mind doesn't know the difference between a synthetic experience and a real one. Have you ever felt your heart race during a movie? It is not due to a real threat, but the perception of one by the mind in response to a very realistic, albeit a synthetic experience. The suspension of reality that happens with things like vivid memories or movies can trick the mind into thinking it is real.

The problem with people who have low self-concepts is that they don't posses a clear enough image of what they want to become, so it is not real enough to their own mind. They don't see their future self very well, and when you don't see your future self clearly, your mind doesn't believe in it. When your mind doesn't believe in something, it usually doesn't happen. The trick to developing a stronger self-concept is to create such strong clarity and realism for where you want to go that it actually becomes real to your mind.

Here is one way to do this: Take a piece of paper and draw a line down the middle (you might need two or even three pieces of paper). At the top of the left-hand side of this paper, write a date from your past when you were happy and very certain about what you were doing. Try to keep this date within the last few years if possible. Underneath that date, down the left hand side of the page, write out bullet points for every single thing you can recall from that date. Some examples would be: how old you were, what kind of work you were doing, what some of your relationships were like and with whom were they with, how many hours you worked, how much did you weigh, what did a typical day in your life look like, what were some of the best memories from around that date, etc. The key is that no detail is too minor or silly. Use as many pages as you need. Before we talk about the next step, you will benefit from this exercise more if you stop reading here and go do this first step now.

Assuming you have filled the left side of your page with very detailed memories from your past, now move your attention to the right side of the page and put a date in the top right corner, similar to the one from the past on the left, and make this date exactly twelve months into the future. Now, for every bullet on the left, your task is to create the same statement on the right, but only in the future. This may seem a little silly, but trust me, it has worked for a great many people over the years.

Continue filling in the items on the right until you have matched them all with the list on the left. As you do this, be your own accountability partner and ask yourself if the statement you have written is as detailed as it could be. Writing "I will make $200,000 next year" is not detailed enough. You need to explain exactly how you will do that, what work will you do, and how will you be rewarded.

What happens when you do this is that you are helping your mind create a synthetic experience—one that is extremely detailed. This is just like comparing a painting and a photo. The photo looks more real because it has much more detail than the painting can capture. If you can learn to do the same thing only with details of your life, then you will be surprised how differently you feel about where you want to go and how much more certainty you have. This process can take place over several hours, days, or can even be something that you revisit many times during a month or more. The more detailed you make it—the more detail you see—the more real it becomes. The next thing you know, you have a pretty solid self-concept for where you are going and what you are to become.

Step Number 4—Developing Role Awareness: Successful people have great understanding for their different roles in life. They know what the role is, how they are to do it, what their objectives are in detail, and have lots of familiarity with their role.

To develop your own role awareness, one of the things you can do is to actually create a role summary for each major role in your life. This role summary should include: the objectives of the role (why are you doing it), the responsibilities of the role, who the role impacts and how, the resources available to you in that role, the obstacles to being successful in that role, the key performance indicators of success in that role (i.e., the metrics you use to judge success), the milestones you should reach and when you should reach them, and finally, the action steps you must take in the next six to twelve months to be successful in that role.

We strongly recommend that you create a role summary for every major role you have in life too, not just professional. One of the things we found was that the most successful people we talked to had this level of understanding and definition for both their personal and professional roles. Most of us have many roles in life (e.g., friend, spouse, daughter or son, brother or sister, church, work, father or mother, etc.). Since it isn't practical to create a role summary like this for every single role you have, we recommend doing this for your most significant roles. My own examples are: father, husband, business owner, and Board member. I have lots of other roles in life, but the ones that impact me the most on a daily basis are those.

Create these role summaries and use them. Put them somewhere where you can see them frequently. Review these role summaries frequently, as often as every month or quarter, depending on how much change these different roles may be experiencing.

Step Number 5—Developing Self-Belief: There are many ways to develop your belief in yourself, but there are three core ways that we use. We will cover the first two in this chapter, but the third is very involved and not something we have time to cover sufficiently here. That said, the first two do not actually focus on your belief in yourself directly, rather they involve focusing on the very things we've been talking about so far (i.e., self-concept and role awareness). What we found is that when people have a very strong self-concept and clear understanding for their roles in life, their level of self-belief goes up. It just makes sense that if you are confident about where you are going and how you are going to get there, your level of belief in your ability to get there increases.

To illustrate this we use the image of a racecar driver. Imagine the negative impact on a racecar driver's level of belief in his ability to win the race if he doesn't know the course very well or isn't very familiar with how to drive the car. It really can be that simple. By understanding and working on the self-concept and role awareness traits we have already discussed, you can make a dramatic positive impact on your level of belief in yourself to win and succeed. With increased self-belief comes increased success. As the old quote from Henry Ford goes, "whether you think you can or you can not—you are probably right."

So, work on Steps Three and Four from above, get greater clarity for where you are going and how you want to get there, and you will directly improve your level of self-belief and your chances of being that much more successful.

The most successful people we met had very secure levels of self-belief. They weren't too high, but they were strong enough to remove self-limiting beliefs and self-doubt. Sure, they questioned themselves. No, they didn't have absolute blind faith in their ability to do anything, but they did have a much higher level of belief than is normally found. Since this is a trait that can be developed, you can develop this high level of belief in yourself too.

Step Number 6—Finding your Genius: The previous steps will make a huge difference in your ability to find your own genius, but there are a few more things you can do to help learn what your greatest talents are.

One thing that we found really helps people start thinking about their natural talents and their genius is to step back and ask themselves what they have really enjoyed doing in life, what kind of things just seem to come naturally to them, what were some of the common denominators in the past successes they enjoyed?

Here are six questions you can ask yourself to help you do that the same:

- What kinds of work and activities make you happy?
- What kinds of things just seem to come effortlessly to you?
- Where is your passion in life or work?
- Can you find any trends in your life among the things you enjoyed the most and where you were the most successful with the least effort?
- What do others say are your greatest natural talents (be honest, not ideal)? Literally ask yourself what others have told you are natural strengths for you. And actually ask people what natural strengths they see in you. One of those we talked to in our work, a PhD who works with Fortune 500 companies to build successful people, has conducted some significant research that proves that the most successful personal development efforts don't happen in a vacuum. The best development occurs when a person gets others involved, has dialogue about what they are trying to do, and asks for input and feedback from those around them on what they think.

The work I describe in this chapter doesn't have to be hard; it just requires that you do it. Most of the time, we find that while these steps can be simple and effective, they are things that many people just don't think about doing. Sometimes simple things are the most effective. Leonardo Da Vinci once said, "Simplicity is the greatest form of sophistication," so do not assume that finding your genius and becoming more successful is a secret that only select people know or some dream that only certain people can achieve. It doesn't have to be hard, and it doesn't have to be mysterious. Give these things a try and see for yourself just how easy it really can be to find your genius and success more frequently and naturally!

Wright

So from everything you've learned during all of this, is there one simple message that people can take away?

Niblick

It would be Hartman's quote, "Stop trying to put in what God left out and instead work with what he put in." What we found about the geniuses we met was that they all shared: a greater level of self-awareness, were more authentic, and they all defined success as happiness and passion found.

If you are reading this, break out of the mold. Don't follow what the common wisdom tells you. Know who you are and be true to it and use that to try and find happiness and points of passion in your life. As hokey as that may sound, the people who have reached the absolute tops in their respective fields tell us this is what they do differently.

Wright

What a great conversation, I have really learned a lot here today and I'm sure that our readers will as well. I really appreciate all the time you've spent here with me today, Jay, to answer all these questions. I know there have been a lot of them. I hope I haven't taken up too much of your time; the answers were certainly fascinating.

Niblick

I really appreciate the invitation, so thank you very much for your time.

Wright

Today we've been talking to Jay Niblick, researcher, entrepreneur, lecturer, and author. He's helped organizations understand the most important, yet least understood aspect of success—decision-making. I'm going to listen to him and I hope you do too.

Jay, thank you so much for being with us today on *Blueprint for Success*.

Niblick

Thank you David, I appreciate it.

About the Author

JAY NIBLICK is founder and CEO of Innermetrix Incorporated. Innermetrix is an international consulting firm helping individuals and organizations large and small leverage the genius of their people in the search for increased performance and profitability.

Jay Niblick
1728 Breezy Ridge Trail
Knoxville TN 37922
Phone: 888.IMX.6803
E-mail: jay@innermetrix.com
www.innermetrix.com

Chapter Eleven

An interview with...

J. C. Melvin

David Wright (Wright)

Today we are speaking with J. C. Melvin. J. C. Melvin is President and CDO (Chief Dreaming Officer) of J.C. Melvin Seminars, Inc. J. C. utilizes his years of experience in the restaurant and bar business and his over twenty-five years in the Real Estate sales business in his unique presentation style.

J. C. Melvin Seminars (established in 1986) is focused on Performance Management on both a personal and business level and acknowledges that the two are closely tied together.

Melvin works with many real estate associations and corporations across the country on leadership, planning, and implementation, all focused on enhancing performance. His book, *I Think I Smell Garlic, A Recipe for Life,* is a focus on the premise that "Life is too short to live the wrong dream."

His work with the United States Agency for International Development had him facilitating programs in Russia, the Ukraine, Romania, and Poland.

In addition, he is considered an expert in Real Estate agency and teaches throughout the country and is revered as one of the premier expert witnesses in the field.

With a clear understanding of "you become what you think about," his workshops are about how to make the right personal choices to enhance your life and career.

J. C., welcome to *Blueprint for Success.*

J. C. Melvin (Melvin)

Thanks, it's wonderful to be here and to contribute with the other fine authors including two of my favorites—Ken Blanchard and Stephen Covey. I was honored to be asked.

Wright

You have a chapter in your book on choices and in it you state: "It's the choices that we make each day that define who we are. It's these choices that express our character to the world." Are you saying that as individuals we always have 100 percent control of the choices we make?

Melvin

Yes, that is exactly what I am saying. It really can be that simple! It starts over each day when we wake up and make the choice to get out of bed . . . or . . . to stay in bed. Then we decide to work out or not work out, to eat healthy or not eat healthy, to be positive, or to be negative.

We are consciously and subconsciously making hundreds of choices each day. Sometimes we make a global choice about something and that global choice or decision stands as an automatic default (subconscious choice) for weeks, months, years, or even a lifetime with no conscious consideration.

Wright

What's an example of a global choice someone might make?

Melvin

Okay, here is a very common global choice: Somewhere in a person's early years (it could be pre-high school, high school, or even college age), the person buys into somebody's words that "money is the root of all evil." Sadly, this likely came from the person's parents or a family member, a schoolteacher, or even from a church, thus it comes with some sort of perceived validity.

The problem is that when the person makes the choice to adopt this as a truth in his or her life, it is re-affirmed in the sub-conscious every day. When people begin to equate wealth and money to evil and apply this misconception to everything, it's global, and the likelihood of their ever achieving wealth in their lifetime is severely diminished.

Wright

Are these people aware of what they are doing to themselves with theses choices?

Melvin

Not on an easily accessible conscious level. In fact, the people we just described in the above example are the same people who cannot understand why they never have any money, why they cannot open their own successful business, or take themselves and their family on that dream vacation.

Wright

How do people get rid of a bad global choice they've made some time ago if they don't even realize it's a stumbling block to their future?

Melvin

First, it requires a conscious choice to do so. Fortunately, one of life's truths is that the door of change is always open. This simply means that if and when people choose to make a change in their life it starts with a conscious thought. I always recommend that people go backward to discover what needs to be changed, for example: A man who has struggled for most of his life financially and never really enjoyed financial success at any significant level makes the decision that he wants to change his life and become super successful.

(When working with both associations and businesses on long-term planning, we often do this exercise and it is very effective.) When I say go backward I mean start with this question: if money was never an issue or concern for you or your family for the rest of your life, what would you do every day?

Wright

What kind of answers do you usually get?

Melvin

The knee-jerk answer is usually, "Oh, I'd travel" or "I'd take my family on a trip to—" or "I'd pay off all my bills and take care of my family." While this is the knee-jerk reaction, we've got to dig a bit more to get to what's really important.

I will now suggest that you have bought all the new cars and houses and paid cash, you have traveled all over the world, the children have big bank accounts set up for their future, and money is still not an issue . . . so . . . now what do you do every day with your life? Another way of asking this question is, "If money were not an issue what would your life be all about?"

Wright

So once you have drilled down, what kind of answers do you get?

Melvin

Interestingly, this is where the spiritual side of human nature begins to show up. Almost 100 percent of those who participate in the exercise come away expressing a desire to help, assist, teach, or contribute to some group or cause in which they believe. It could be to work with underprivileged children or people with certain types of disabilities or to raise funds to fight cancer or any number of other causes.

I know a woman who believed if children were exposed to making beautiful music at a young age it could and would greatly enhance their self-esteem, so she focused on assisting children to learn to play various instruments and perform beautiful music. She believed these children had a much better chance to grow into confident, creative adults.

Wright

Are you suggesting that knowing the answer to the "what would you do every day" question will make you successful?

Melvin

Yes, although it's only the beginning. Think about this for just one minute: most people on the planet have never done this exercise and they don't teach it in school at any level. What most children are taught is to go to school, get a good education so that you can get a good job, and become whatever the focus is—waitress, teacher, doctor, lawyer, contractor, or any number of other occupations.

Please don't misunderstand me—there is nothing wrong with any of these jobs or professions. The point is that "Big Thinking" is not taught in our current system.

If a person wants to be super successful, he or she will end up in the top 3 percent of income earners in the country. In order to do that, the person must think bigger than what is taught in our school system. The exercise above is the door of change that allows a person to begin thinking bigger.

Wright

Why is completing the exercise so important?

Melvin

It is for clarity of purpose. Most people go through their entire life not knowing the answer to that question, let alone having a personal mission statement. Hence, most people lack clarity in their life as to what they are all about and tend to go in whatever direction the wind takes them. It is that lack of clarity that is a major contributor to high school dropouts, our prisons being so full, child and spousal abuse, and even homelessness.

Wright

How long should the exercise take for an individual to complete?

Melvin

When dealing with individuals, about 5 percent have already given some thought to this and are able to answer on the spot. I usually recommend for most to take a weekend or a week giving thought to what they would do for an hour or so each day, again with money being no object.

I also suggest that it is a personal thing. What I mean by this is that the answer to this question is not what your spouse would do or what you and your spouse would do, it is strictly about you and what you would do given the opportunity. I've had some analytical types take up to three weeks to put down what they would do given the opportunity.

It is really quite a serious question to ponder and the time needed will vary with the individual.

Wright

The question seems to be far different than the standard question of what do I want to be when I grow up.

Melvin

Absolutely—the question we deal with in going through school is what do I want to be when I grow up? That's a conscious decision we are taught to make and then we put the things in motion that are necessary to achieve that goal.

The questions we are asking now is not only what do I want to be; but rather, who am I and what's my passion in life? What legacy will I leave?

Wright

Okay, so now they understand themselves and their personal mission more. Is this the catalyst for becoming successful?

Melvin

Yes it is! With this clarity, everything becomes easier. Their life's mission is now a known factor that has been brought to an absolute conscious level. Just as in preparing for a degree or a career, they can now set in place the plan necessary to achieve their life's mission.

Wright

What about that bad global choice made about money being evil?

Melvin

Perfect—now it's time to come back to our situation. First, we removed money as an issue to determine the personal mission in life. Now we have some clarity about ourselves and what we are all about. We must continue going backward and ask ourselves, "What needs to happen for me to put myself in the situation where I can freely do what I've determined is my life's mission?"

Part of the answer to this will invariably come back to creating a financial position to ensure the end result.

Making the assumption that the personal contribution you've chosen is positive, you can begin to dissect and dispel the notion that money is the root of all evil. We now realize that in order to achieve our mission, which is good, will require money. It is not a bad thing—it just is what it is. You can begin to adjust your thinking and understanding that money is only a tool like any other tool.

Wright

JC, in your book you suggest that everyone has the choice to change his or her mindset and attitude if the person wants to. Is that right?

Melvin

Correct. We can look at well-publicized books and movies of the day that reinforce this concept such as *The Secret,* for example. On a different note, one of my favorite quotes is, *"The greatest discovery of my generation is that a human being can alter his life by altering his attitudes."* This quote comes from a modern American philosopher by the name of William James who, by the way, was born in 1842 (1842–1910).

The truth is that the only secret out there is that we are what we think about, and thought is the beginning of all creation. It's about focus and what a person chooses to focus on!

In the example thus far, our person had both a misguided concept that money was evil and at the same time was focused on his (or her) constant lack of money. With the clarity of the person's mission and real desire in life, the focus can shift away from negative concepts and conditions of lack to positively achieving the individual's mission in the spirit of abundance!

Wright

Can a person's attitude change that quickly by simply making the personal choice to change his or her thinking?

Melvin

Making the personal choice to change is the beginning. There must be some commitment on the part of the person wanting to change. Depending on how deep-rooted a person is in his or her past thinking and how open minded the person is willing to be makes all the difference.

Let's not refer to past thinking as negative thinking and beliefs but rather as "default beliefs."

It is work to change a habit and we must understand that default beliefs are a habit that we have reaffirmed both consciously and sub-consciously for years. Most people's default beliefs focus on negatives like money is bad, the world is evil, the educational system is no good, I hate my job, my marriage is in turmoil, I don't have enough money, I'm too fat, I'm too skinny, I never get any breaks, etc.

It is very easy to maintain such a default belief system because most of the world's media reinforce it across the globe morning, noon, and night with headlines of war, economic doom, murder, terrorism, and every other kind of black cloud. So, in essence, we have been feeding ourselves and our default belief system every day with the wrong food.

The work part of the process is to take the action necessary to begin feeding our mind and body positive energy and thoughts daily which in turn change our actions. This will cause a change in results, which in turn creates a more positive attitude. This will cause us to seek out and feed ourselves with more positive thoughts.

Wright

Although the concept sounds simple, it also sounds like changing the way one thinks could be difficult. What advice would you give to a person who sincerely wants to move to a whole new level in his or her thinking and life?

Melvin

That's a great point and the toughest part of changing the way we think is not the decision to change, although that in itself is very difficult for some. The toughest part about thinking differently is creating a new habit in the way we view and deal with thought.

Our brain considers thousands of thoughts per hour and tens to hundreds of thoughts per minute. Remember, for most of these common thoughts we already have a programmed default belief system in place that processes these thoughts and files them.

The key element of thinking differently is to short circuit the programmed default belief system that has been running our thought department. Yes, we all have a thought department in our brain and it is the single most responsible area for the person we are and the attitude we demonstrate to the world.

With tens to hundreds of thoughts per minute being generated we must first focus on the important thoughts. In the beginning, it can seem overwhelming but to start with; simply pick the thoughts that you feel are important.

Wright

How does one "short circuit" a thought to change the way one thinks?

Melvin

Now we are down to the nuts and bolts of the process. Let's take, for example, a lady who is overweight and has been for years. She gets up in the morning, walks to the bathroom, and sees herself in the mirror and a fleeting thought passes across her mind: *"God, I'm fat"* or *"I'm big"* or *"Wow"* or *"I think I look bigger today than yesterday"* or any number of other thoughts. The trick is for her to not process that thought the same way (by default) that she has been processing it in the past. If she determines that the weight thing is important to her and this is an important thought she wishes to deal with, she must put the brakes on the thought department's normal handling of this thought and *consciously* contribute a different position statement regarding the thought to the thought department. In other words, this is where she needs to short circuit the old standard default thought and replace it with a different thought.

Since we know she wants to get more positive and change her belief system, here is where she must select a new conscious thought that is in her mind's best interest and insert it. The new thought might be, *"I have a beautiful face"* or *"I am a powerful person"* or *"I love being alive"* or *"You are a wonderful and powerful person"* or *"I am healthy and powerful"* or *"Wow, you look good"* or whatever positive thought she wishes to insert.

In doing this replacement work, at first it may seem silly, however, I suggest that it is verbalized aloud, look back at one's self in the mirror and verbalize it again. If it seems funny I encourage enjoying a good laugh.

Now each and every time throughout the day and evening that negative thinking attempts to run across the mind, insert the new conscious thought.

It will take a couple of weeks or more to replace the old thought and it will require *conscious effort* each and every time the thought comes up.

The key here is to be aware that your mind only knows what you feed it, so feed it positive thoughts!

Wright

How many key thoughts can a person work on at a time, for instance, over a two or three week period?

Melvin

Wonderful question and with literally thousands of thoughts per day to choose from, my recommendation is that a person start by choosing themes that he or she wishes to work on or ideologies the person wishes to change. For example, if people know that they are negative and pessimistic about everything in their world, from personal to business to family, they may want to make a commitment to stop and focus their conscious effort on negative thought, replacing it with positive.

Another example might be for people who seem to be angry all the time and mad at the world. Usually these people are mad and/or disappointed with themselves, but are throwing negative energy outward at the world. They have not, in many cases, discovered that they are mad at themselves. If these angry people have truly made a commitment to change, they must realize that only they have influence and control over their emotions.

Another truth of life is that we all have emotional freedom. That is to say, we each get to choose how we react to things in our world, whatever they may be. Once this truth is known, we must short-circuit our thought department's process every time we begin to default to anger.

In this situation, we may need to deal with the ideology behind the anger each time it arises. For example, a driver on the road did not signal to turn forcing you to step on your brakes in a hurry. The angry person might start muttering under his or her breath or openly about what a jerk the other driver was. The angry person might actually get emotionally worked up about it. The question here is how can we allow the actions of someone else to play such a big role in our lives? The realization is this: if we choose to invest our emotional capital into this outside influence now and/or on a regular basis, then we are acknowledging that outside sources "control" how we feel and react to life.

It is imperative that we adjust our emotional point of view and take back control of our emotional capital. In other words, the fact that the other driver did not properly signal cannot become a major focus. If anything, the conscious effort in this example to short circuit the default thought process has got to change the paradigm of our emotional point of view. Perhaps when we feel any anger about this coming on, we've got to say to ourselves, *"Wow, I'm an alert and good driver"* or *"I am grateful that my car and its brakes are in good condition"* or *"I'll say a prayer for that person, I hope they'll be okay."* In any case, the thought and emotional point of view must change and this process must be followed each time the anger pops up.

Initiating change can be challenging and I suggest people make this effort a fun experience. Don't be afraid to laugh at yourself. If you can get your arms around how funny it is that an outside influence could possibly control your inner feelings, then when you find it happening (and you will), you've got to laugh at yourself. This mind set is all a part of changing the way you think.

Wright

JC, it sounds like what you are saying is that once a person decides to make the personal choice to enhance or change his or her life or thinking, the work to do so runs minute to minute on a daily basis?

Melvin

Yes, however, let's change the mindset of what you just said in your question. Rather than say the "work" to do so runs minute to minute, let's say that the "opportunity" to make changes and improve runs minute to minute. This in itself has a more fun, optimistic, and exciting feel to it since most people default the word work to something that is not so much fun.

Wright

So in relation to the rest of the book with the other chapters on leadership, success, customer service, courage, and the rest, making the personal choice of how to think and be positive is a major key?

Melvin

Not only is it a major key, the choice of how we think is what makes all the difference in what we pursue in life and business. The person who elects to continue thinking as he or she always has will continue to reap the same things that the thought process has brought him or her in the past.

We all know someone who is the victim of misfortune. We know people who are victims each and every day of their lives. There is always major drama going on and it is never their fault. We refer to these people as being on a victim trip. When we take a look at these people we can see clearly that it all stems from how they think and how they choose to spend their emotional capital. In other words, it's their choice.

Wright

You keep using the term "emotional capital" as though it's something we all have to spend. Will you explain that?

Melvin

Sure, in my newest book, which deals with emotional freedom, we discuss two areas of life in detail: one is emotional freedom and the other is financial freedom. What we learn through the study of emotional freedom is that nobody but you can control how you feel emotionally. It is an individual choice, plain and simple.

In December of 2005 my wife was diagnosed with stage three plus ovarian cancer. This is a rather blunt and powerful fact to be made aware of. How she chose to deal with it emotionally was up to her. She chose to deal with it in a very positive manner. While I tended to initially default to being an emotional wreck, she chose to get extremely positive. She told me not to worry—it was simply not in her plans to become a cancer victim. She met with all the necessary doctors, changed her diet, had two major surgeries, six months of chemotherapy, and is now cancer free. This was very powerful because the doctors had advised me she might not come out of the first surgery!

In the example of my wife, she could have spent her emotional capital by becoming an emotional wreck, being a victim, or giving up and throwing in the towel. Instead she chose to invest her emotional capital with a powerful and positive mindset.

Both the surgeon and the oncologist were in awe and used the word "miracle" six months after the fact.

Needless to say, her emotional strength gave me a whole new perspective and caused my emotional state to become much more positive and supportive and together we moved beyond that temporary setback. My wife is also my business partner and we just completed a seven-country speaking trip. She has now run for and been elected to the board of a 16,000 member Real Estate association.

On a side note I should mention here that my wife and I are both believers in the pooling of positive energy and prayer to create powerful results. We had a variety of friends and business associates who included her name in their prayer groups. Although we both happen to have been raised Catholic, we had Mormons, Jews, Christian Scientists, Religious Scientists, Protestants, Catholics, Muslims, and I think we even had some atheists praying for her!

Wright

What about the people who seem to be unhappy with their lives and appear unmotivated to do anything to change their situation?

Melvin

The short answer is this: it is their personal choice to stay right where they are, period. You mention motivation or the lack of motivation—everybody has motivation, it's just that some motivation is what we perceive as negative and some we perceive as positive. Even the couch potato has motivation to sit on the couch and watch television. While many may look at this person and say, "They have no motivation to change their life," the truth is that they do have motivation—to lie around the house and watch television. The real question is why? On another side note here, I will suggest that we need to be careful to stay out of judgment regarding people like this. Remember, it is their life and it is their choice. Ironically, it's not uncommon that people like these are the ones saying, "I wish I could do this" or "I wish I could do that."

Most people who are truly inspired and thus motivated to think differently and take productive action to produce desired results, tend to avoid uninspired people. Inspired people are much more attracted to other inspired people. This is known as the law of attraction and it comes right back to you—you get (or attract) whatever you think about.

The question for all of us to consider is what is our inspiration in life? The person who seems unmotivated probably just lacks the inspiration that stimulates positive motivation and productive action. My bottom line answer to your question about the people who seem unhappy and unmotivated is that they have made the personal choice to be that way.

Wright

Okay, let's say that somebody has picked up this book and he or she has either been totally negative and wants to change or he or she has had some success and are looking to move to a new level in life. Where does this person start?

Melvin

People in this situation have already started just by the fact that they are reading this right now. They should be commended for being in possession of the book and understand that it's not an accident they have it! Someway, somehow, their personal thought process led them to be in possession of this book whether they bought it or someone gave it to them as a gift, either way it is the law of attraction at work.

The reading of this book is productive action and I would encourage them to continue their research, reading helpful materials, and taking more productive action to either determine their life mission (inspiration) or to reinforce their actions in the direction that will lead to the accomplishment of their life's mission.

Understand that one piece of research leads to another—one action leads to another and it's all good.

Mo Anderson, the woman I spoke of earlier in this chapter who had a simple passion to teach music to kids is now the vice chairman of the board and a cultural icon of one of the largest Real Estate firms in the world. She now has a positive influence on over 78,000 associates and counting and is impacting their families as well, bringing the number of those she is touching to hundreds of thousands of people. She has also been monumental in the establishing of a charity foundation that assists those in need to the tune of millions of dollars each year. This woman was born into the family of a poor tenant farmer in Okalahoma and struggled to obtain her degree that allowed her to teach music to youngsters in school. Mo would tell you to follow your heart and trust your inner faith and instincts. Mo is a devout Christian and is committed to her belief both privately and publicly.

Wright

Regarding personal choices with the people and the organizations you have worked with, what would you site as the major difference between thinking average and thinking great?

Melvin

I would say it has everything to do with a person's belief in themselves and their mission. It all comes right back to the way we think and whether we are feeding ourselves with positive mental and emotional nourishment or have succumbed to the easy to find, yet damaging low vibrating cycle of life.

The greats are committed to what inspires them and they seem to possess much more clarity of vision. Another interesting characteristic about great people is their simple gratefulness for life and the opportunity to live it!

A huge difference exists between the concept of scarcity and the concept of abundance. People who live in abundance tend to be more positive and believe in abundance whether talking about love, commitment, money, or possibilities. People who live in scarcity tend to be more pessimistic and dwell in lack or a perceived scarcity of love money, commitment, and possibilities.

Greatness and clarity of vision, regardless of the mission, requires information, knowledge, and passion. The more open people are to their spiritual self and following their heart, the more likely they are to live in abundance. In any event, it is a personal choice.

Wright

Do the way you think and the thoughts you feed your mind have direct connections with the level of your emotional vibration?

Melvin

Absolutely—it has everything to do with the level of vibration. It is really very simple. Spiritually and emotionally we will always attract other things that are vibrating at the same or similar frequency as we are. This is the exact reason why it is so important to vibrate at the highest frequency possible at any given moment.

This is a great question and a critical point regarding the choices we make. If it's true that we get what we focus on and the more positive we are, the more we vibrate at a higher frequency, it stands to reason that we would want to feed ourselves with all the positive energy we could get our hands on.

When we make the conscious decision to get more positive, we are also making the decision to live at a higher frequency, even if we don't understand it or know what that means. This will change our life and our world.

Wright

Now it sounds like you are getting into the philosophy that people can do anything they want in life, and all they have to do is think about it. Is that right?

Melvin

It really comes down to the possibilities a person can see and the belief he or she has. Changing the way we think increases the possibilities we can see and expands our belief library. This in turn enhances our overall ability to think bigger about things that we may have never before considered.

Getting anything we want in life however, does require more than just thought, it requires what we call "productive action." The more we feed the thought process with positive input and the more we begin to focus on what our personal clarity is in life, the more actively we will pursue the productive action that will bring about change in our lives.

The truth is that it all starts with thought, so that's not a bad place to focus personal energy to begin with.

Wright

You mentioned earlier that we should stay out of judgment of other people. Why is that important?

Melvin

It's important if it's our personal desire to learn and grow. When we stumble into the judgmental role and stay there, we are generally comparing all others to ourselves. In doing this we tend to set ourselves up as something that we are not and this hampers growth.

I have a friend who is a multi-millionaire. In fact, he is one of the most successful people in history in the network marketing business. His name is Richard Kall. He was originally introduced to the multi-level marketing business by a mechanic in greasy overalls who asked him at an auto repair shop if he had financial freedom. Richard Kall was one of those people (and still is) who was learning-based and open minded.

Had my friend, Richard, been judgmental at that time and said to himself, "Who in the heck does this grease monkey think he's talking to?" or "I am obviously way more successful than he will ever be," the conversation would have gone no further. Instead, Richard told his wife they needed to attend a meeting. As the story goes, when they approached the house where the meeting was to be held, the house on the left and the house on the right were both in foreclosure and looked horrible. The one they were going into looked even worse.

The point is that Mr. Kall, even though he was extremely successful at the time (in 1978) in the insurance and Real Estate business, he was not judgmental and he did attend the meeting with the mechanic.

Today Mr. Kall enjoys a massive income in excess of hundreds of thousands of dollars per month from that industry. He is also an owner and the chairman of the board for one of the most innovative Internet communication companies on the planet called Helloworld.

He is a loving, caring man who freely gives back to his associates and community on a daily basis. He travels the world assisting and training others who are interested in building financial freedom through network marketing. In fact he authored, *The Book on Network Marketing* (published by Nemanity, LLC).

We all have the ability to learn from others, so the long answer to your question is to be careful about being judgmental of others especially when doing so shuts off the possibility of learning and growing from the experience.

This is all a part of thinking differently and moving away from our existing "default beliefs."

Wright

For my last question let me ask this: is there a time when the process of thinking differently begins to get easier?

Melvin

Yes, changing our mindset and making better personal choices becomes easier as we focus on it and do it more and more. The exciting part is making the commitment to change and taking those first few steps. A friend to all of us, Wayne Dyer, said, "If you change the way you look at things, the things you look at change." This is 100 percent true and the personal choices we make in life are responsible for who we are and where we are in life.

Simply stated, trust in yourself and have faith that you want to make some changes and move to a higher vibration and/or a different direction in your life. Once you open your heart to the universe and sincerely put out there what you desire, the law of attraction will naturally begin to bring those things to you.

My recommendations: learn, grow, and enjoy the ride!

About the Author

J. C. MELVIN is President and CDO (Chief Dreaming Officer) of J.C. Melvin Seminars, Inc. JC utilizes his years of experience in the restaurant and bar business and his over twenty-five years in the Real Estate Sales business in his unique presentation style.

J.C. Melvin Seminars (established in 1986) is focused on Performance Management on both an individual and corporate level and acknowledges that the two are closely tied together.

Melvin works with many Real Estate associations and growth corporations across the country on leadership, planning, and implementation, all focused on enhancing performance. His book, *I Think I Smell Garlic, A Recipe for Life,* is a focus on the premise that "Life is too short to live the wrong dream."

His work with the United States Agency for International Development had him facilitating programs in Russia, the Ukraine, Romania, and Poland.

In addition he is revered as a top expert in the field of Real Estate agency and is often called upon as an expert witness.

JC speaks and facilitates throughout the United States and Europe on Performance Management.

With a clear understanding of "you become what you think about," his workshops are about how to make the right personal choices to enhance one's life and career.

His topic's include, *It's my life but whose in charge?, You've got to be kidding,* and *I know I said it but I didn't really mean it!*

J. C. Melvin
J.C. Melvin Seminars, Inc
702.454.9822
jc@jcmelvin.com
www.JCMelvin.com

Chapter Twelve

Rand Golletz

David Wright (Wright)

Today we're talking with Rand Golletz. Many coaches and consultants who work with business leaders "talk the talk," but Rand also "walks the walk"! Rand has spent twenty-five years achieving significant results working in large organizations. As the youngest officer of a Fortune 100 company, he led his company's sales development efforts. Later, as Senior Vice-President and Chief Marketing and Sales Officer of another Fortune 100 firm, he led the charge for a multi-billion dollar brand.

Rand's experience also includes the titles of CEO and COO for companies with hundreds of millions of dollars of revenue as well as director and practice leader for the strategy consulting practice of a top ten world-wide consultancy. Today Rand works with corporate leaders and business owners to develop and sustain the focus, discipline, and momentum they require for professional and personal success. His book, *Redefining Type A*, will be published in 2009.

Rand, welcome to *Blueprint for Success!*

Rand Golletz (Golletz)

Thanks, David. With an introduction like that I can't wait to hear what I have to say!

Wright

Did your mother write it? (Laughter)

Golletz

Exactly!

Wright

You work with executives and business owners. Do you find that your background helps you to help them? If so, in what ways?

Golletz

It's funny; when I started my business about eight years ago, after being a CEO in the corporate world, I wasn't sure what my niche would be. I found that when I intersected what I brought to the table from my experience with what executives were looking for—someone who saw the journey between point A and point B as a straight line—then I hit my sweet spot. So I now work with a lot of executives who are Type A—impatient leaders who don't have a lot of free time and don't want to get real wrapped up in process for its own sake. These are people who are looking to achieve results with the help of a "been there/done that" kind of person. So, yes, the kind of person who wants advice and solutions benefits a great deal from what I bring to the table. Very few people in my line of work bring the type of experience that I bring to the consulting and coaching profession. I've actually run companies, and that's a *huge* benefit for my clients.

Wright

You have frequently said that a lot of the "leadership development" work that companies do is useless. Would you elaborate on that?

Golletz

Let's say that I'm the CEO of an organization and my CFO "David" doesn't have a whole lot of "people skills." Typically, when someone has a hard time with collaboration or doesn't delegate well, we aggregate those things under the broad heading of people skills. As his boss, I'll be looking through catalogs to find a workshop for David. Subsequently, I may identify the four-day Harvard workshop titled *How to Give David Better People Skills*, and we send David to the workshop expecting that when he comes back he'll be spiritually evolved and perfect in every way.

Then David comes back from the workshop and gets back into the work environment and doesn't get the kind of support and affirmation he needs to practice the new things he learned. Pretty soon it's business as usual—David is back to doing business the way David always did business. We then realize that we wasted fifteen thousand dollars. *Countless* companies do that!

Another instructive example: I got a call from a large organization about three years ago to work with an executive. Apparently this guy had a bit of an impulse control problem because two weeks earlier in the middle of his own staff meeting, he had put the heel of his shoe through his own computer screen! Now the CEO and the CFO of the organization were looking for an executive coach to work with this guy to impart maybe a little more "effective" way to manage and lead. My first question was, "Why is this guy still working here?" And yet they were willing to spend countless thousands of dollars hoping to "fix" the guy. My response to executives who are looking to "fix" someone is, "If you want somebody fixed, send him or her to a veterinarian." By the time somebody is forty or fifty years old a lot of a person's attributes of personality and character are pretty hardwired. In this case, the guy would have benefited far more from psychotherapy and medication than from working with an executive coach.

I run across those kinds of examples *all* the time in companies of all sizes and types, where the assumption is: if you are bringing in an expert from out of town or you send somebody to a workshop, there's going to be dramatic improvement in executive performance. That's not always the case.

This leads me to the following: I believe that four elements or categories comprise or create confidence, which is the real key for performance and success. Those elements are: *knowledge, skills, talents,* and *personal attributes.* You need to understand and be able to distinguish among those and identify the best route to their development in order to have an effective approach to leadership development in any organization.

Wright

You just raised some interesting distinctions. So what exactly are the differences among those elements—knowledge, skills, talents, and attributes?

Golletz

Knowledge is about the "what." It's the level of learning of concepts and facts, so it's the kind of information that you can pick up reading books or attending seminars. You'll learn the "what," but not the "how." I could read a book on airplane mechanics, but you don't want me on a runway working on that airplane people are actually going to fly in, because I've never done that! So that's knowledge, and that's necessary, but alone it's insufficient—it's just a start.

Skills, contrasted with knowledge, are strengths at performing specific tasks. For example, I knew a surgeon who had written a number of textbooks on orthopedic surgery. He was a recognized expert, yet he wasn't great in the operating room. His reputation was as a guy who knew what to do, but when it came to being a "cutter," he wasn't the best. So skills are typically developed with practice. They're strengths at "doing."

I characterize talents as genetic strengths. The example I use is my wife. My wife is a terrific woman; she's also tone deaf. I could spend hundreds of thousands of dollars for her to work with Andrea Bocelli, but she's still going to be tone deaf. She can never aspire to being an opera singer. Another example: one of my sisters-in-law is head of clinical statistics for a medium-sized biotech company. I am convinced that when she was born she was computing! So we are born with predispositions toward strength in specific areas. While we have to work on their development during our lives, they are strengths that are, to some degree, hardwired.

The last area, and this is really tricky, is what I call personal attributes. Those are characteristics of personality, morality, and character that are developed in childhood, particularly through parental love and support. Those can be further developed later in life with patience, persistence, practice, and reinforcement, but to a large degree they are imparted in our youth. Courage, discipline, endurance, and persistence—the kinds of things that give us leverage in some of those other areas—come as a result of our upbringing.

The bottom-line: It's not quite as easy as reading a book or going to a workshop. You've got to know what the issues are in order to focus your resources effectively when it comes to development.

Wright

What strengths are embodied by the most effective managerial leaders?

Golletz

A lot of pages, time, energy, and money have been dedicated to the differences and distinctions between management and leadership. Traditionally we think of management as planning, organizing, staffing, and controlling—the hard skills. And we think of leadership as vision and aligning constituents around the vision, as well as inspiration. My clients, the kind of people who come to me, are people who need to both lead *and* manage. They have to inspire, but they also have to perspire. They have to set direction and build consensus, but they also have to develop plans and make sure that results happen. They have to delegate without abdicating. They have to be able to change the tires on the car while it's moving at sixty miles per hour!

So, I look at effective managerial leadership as the capacity to create value, consistently and over time, for all the constituents of the organization without compromising away the interests of any of them in the process. That requires a number of strengths in order to be effective. I'll go through these fairly quickly, and I'll only get into detail on a couple of them.

The first is a strong business orientation and understanding. Effective business managerial leaders need to have real outstanding business acumen and judgment. They need to think of the needs of all stakeholders. They need to achieve results without excuses. They've got to have a clear understanding of the anatomy and competitive dynamics of the business. They've got to believe in leverage, focusing on the most critical areas; they've got to balance short and long-term priorities across all of their constituencies.

The second attribute is the inclination to assume accountability, initiative, and leadership. They've got to have a strong desire to lead, and they've got to assume initiative even in the absence of formal authority. They've got to keep apprised of the important operating details of the business without impairing empowerment. They've got to be assertive without being overwhelming. They've got to build a competitive team focused on creating value rather than bureaucracy. They've got to be merit driven rather than politically driven, and so on.

A few of the other characteristics: They've got to energize teams. They've got to be able to transform their organizations, which involves having clear vision and the courage to change rather than just running their organizations. They've got to have a raging impatience with the status quo; they've also got to have outstanding judgment and action regarding people; they've got to be curious; they've got to have a high level of emotional intelligence. Courage, persistence, endurance, integrity, and perseverance don't hurt either!

So it isn't easy, my friends.

Wright

Can a leader be effective without all of those elements?

Golletz

Sure, nobody has them all. Sometimes organizations call me to help them build super-leaders, and that just never happens. Focusing on and leveraging strength is one of my obsessions. As you mentioned, a number of years ago I led the strategy consulting practice for a large consulting firm. Part of my challenge was helping corporate executives think strategically. As a practical matter, strategic plans are frequently an inappropriate linear extrapolation of the past, while real strategic thinking requires vision and creativity.

In those days I would take clients through a SWOT analysis—strengths, weaknesses, opportunities, and threats. As executives detailed their organizations' current strengths and weaknesses, as well as their current and prospective competitive challenges, one ultimate objective was to develop plans that would enable their organizations to increase existing strengths and leverage strengths rather than improve weaknesses. Invariably, most executives wanted to focus on improving organizational weaknesses. Their perspective was, "Why should I spend our time doing anything about our strengths because they're already strengths?" The fact is, to quote Peter Drucker, "The primary objective of managers is to make strength productive." Most executives spend way too much time improving weaknesses and not enough time leveraging strengths. With the environment of hyper-competition that exists today, by the time an organization or a person builds a new core competence, it will likely be irrelevant. So leveraging existing strengths is almost always a less expensive and more effective proposition than building or buying new ones.

Today I spend most of my time helping individual executives in organizations figure out what it is they themselves do well, and then how to leverage those strengths against opportunities rather than focus in on the development of weaknesses until they become slightly stronger weaknesses.

That's the long answer to your question. But no, nobody is equally good at all of those things—everybody wants to improve their weaknesses, and much of the time that effort is a waste of resources.

Wright

If pressed, what would you say is the most important strength for a managerial leader?

Golletz

If pressed, I would say "objectivity." Most people in most situations convince themselves that they're always being objective when they're not. Here's the reason: Each of us is burdened with a unique worldview based on our individual life experiences, and along the road we subconsciously conclude that our own worldview represents objective reality. Then later in our lives as we process information, we begin to edit out information that doesn't conform to our preconceptions. At the same time we aggressively seek out and consume information that affirms our perspectives. That's why it's tough to "teach an old dog new tricks." At some point, a lot of people develop psychic sclerosis—hardening of the attitudes. Really effective executives *don't* do that. These people—these really super-performers— routinely challenge their own thinking. They build mechanisms to make sure that their own perspective is assaulted. They stay fresh and intellectually curious. They don't become prisoners of their preconceptions.

Wright

You're writing a book entitled *Redefining Type A*. So what's with the title?

Golletz

I covered a little bit of this earlier, but first of all, it's a great title isn't it? It's really about being effective without damaging yourself and others along the way. It's about achieving planned results versus the exercise of power for its own sake. It's about learning from mistakes; I think that's called "wisdom." A lot of businesspeople, even those you or I would identify as ostensibly successful, have a hard time with nuance or subtlety. I say keep your edge, but deploy it wisely, consistently, and in a way that is going to benefit everybody including yourself.

Wright

Easier said than done, I'd say.

Golletz

Whoa, my goodness!

Wright

I was just thinking of myself.

Golletz

You know, from my perspective the new Type A—the effective Type A—does three things very well. Those are embodied in an admonition that I use with clients: "Get real! Get tough! And get going!"

Wright

And so what do you mean by that admonition?

Golletz

"Get real" is about being objective. We talked about that earlier—differentiating between facts and intuition and dealing with what is instead of contrived or concocted reality.

"Get going" simply means that results only come after relevant action. Our friend Anthony Robbins says that, "Life rewards action." I really believe that life rewards *relevant* action. There is a difference between action and activity. Real legitimate action must achieve a planned result.

Regarding "get tough," the old Type A had a hard time distinguishing between tough-mindedness on the one hand and hard-headedness on the other. So the new Type A's are tough-minded without being hardheaded.

Wright

So toughness isn't harsh or arbitrary. Will you site a few examples to distinguish tough-mindedness from hard-headedness?

Golletz

I could go on forever, but I'll just give you a few. Most managers and entrepreneurs talk about the importance of collaboration. When it comes to execution, however, managers' behavior often violates their own espoused beliefs because getting things done is a higher priority than getting people to work together. Tough-minded leaders recognize that.

Another example: Tough-minded managers take action that achieves planned results. Hardheaded managers frequently take action that does nothing but solidify their authority and personal power.

A third example: Tough-minded mangers select people for jobs and for promotions based upon past performance and position-relevant strengths. Hardheaded managers frequently select people whose views and perspectives replicate their own. I discuss a lot more examples in detail in my one-hour presentation titled "Tough-Minded Leadership." (This has been a paid political announcement.)

Wright

You talk about the priority for business leaders to answer the big questions. So what are the big questions?

Golletz

Big questions are the precursors for success in any area of life. Often times they require a high level of introspection and reflection. Most people have a hard time with really compelling questions because they disrupt things. They open the door to ambiguity and chaos. As soon as we ask a big question, one that we don't necessarily know the answer to, all bets are off and all possibilities are open. So in a business context, a big question is one that can change a company's direction. For a business leader it's one that can change the direction of his or her life.

Here's an example: I ask many people with whom I work to write their leadership story. Two of the big questions I ask are, "Who are you?" and "Who do you want to be?" For many or most of them (and almost always the guys—I find that women have an easier time with these than men—don't ask me to get into that), they want more precise questions. They are not comfortable; they get agitated. They have to engage in a level of thinking and feeling that they haven't experienced before, or at least in a long time, because they are asking themselves big questions. Often, they keep probing to try to get a more precise question from me, but I just keep reneging in order to compel them to really look inside and get at the core of who they are.

Wright

You talk about the difference in leadership styles. I've done several books on leadership with some of the greatest minds. I get the idea here when you're talking about leadership and management—I know the difference is vision and that sort of thing, but most people talk about leadership and management separately. What you're saying, if I understand you correctly, is that people who are like I am—those who lead—have to manage at the same time. Correct?

Golletz

Exactly. Something happened in the late 1980s and through the 1990s that I believe was the unintended consequence of the preeminence we gave to leadership over management. We began to denigrate the priority of effective management. As we aspired to be much more effective and evolved leaders and to demonstrate the behaviors of effective leadership—building consensus, developing collaboration, aligning people around objectives so that they voluntarily achieved what their organizations wanted them to achieve rather than through some kind of a coercive model—we began to assume that management was no longer important. That's just hogwash. Effective management has to continue to exist in organizations, and a lot of organizations found that out in the 1990s as they discarded their management training and management education and the notion that planning, organizing, staffing, and controlling were still important. We still have to do those things. I think the evolved managerial leader is much more effective now at bringing people on board, but we still have to manage our organizations. We still have to achieve planned results, and we still have to develop and implement corrective actions in real time when we're off target.

Wright

I remember reading management books, and I believe I understood the idea that I was supposed to be one or the other, but the truth of the matter is, sometimes it takes me a week to come up with a vision that will change something in a company and the next two years trying to get it done through effective management.

Golletz

I know a lot of leaders for whom vision is really hallucination. You know—lofty, philosophical pronouncements that are unsupported by strength or driven by action. I would much rather have the effective execution of a vision with lower aspirations than to have a vision that was nothing more than a hallucination without the tools in place to assure its execution. I'm sure you've found that in your business as well. At some point, vision has to devolve into relevant work and the achievement of planned results.

Wright

We are all really pressed for time. Many people seem to be working, or at least they are in contact or reachable by work 24/7. You work with leaders to use time more effectively. Will you give our readers a condensed version of that?

Golletz

Dr. Stephen Covey talks about effective time management within the context of a two-by-two box matrix. On one axis is Importance and on the other axis is Urgency. He says that the area a lot of us have a problem in is the "Important but not Urgent" quadrant. Activities in that area include self-development, the development of others, planning, visioning. I call them "enduring priorities." Much of the time I find that my clients initially have a hard time prioritizing the stuff that is urgent, but not important.

Here's an example: I frequently have my clients do what I call a "Calendar Audit." I will ask them to go back about sixty days and to categorize all of their time in one of a number of buckets. I don't use Dr. Covey's Four-Quadrant Matrix for this—I have my own categories. I have them bucket all of their time, except the time they spend sleeping. I find that leaders—right up to the CEOs of Fortune 500 companies—really don't have a good idea of how they spend their time or whether they are aligning their time with what they say their priorities are. So, at the end of that period of time, we'll take a look at how they spend their time versus what they espouse their priorities to be.

I had a client in New York City a couple of years ago who was the CEO of an investment bank. He was your proto-typical, hard-charging Type A—a cigar-chomping, suspenders-snapping, Gucci-wearing plutocrat. This guy spent seventy or eighty hours a week in the office, and yet he constantly talked about his family as his number one priority. Now, my suspicion was that his family was not his number one priority, but it made him feel better to say that. So we went through this calendar exercise. What we found was over a period of about three months he had spent a total of six hours with his family! The next couple of weeks he spent trying to justify that. Once we got beyond that he spent more time in the areas that he espoused as priorities and less time where he *had* been spending his time.

We all like to delude ourselves into thinking that we are focusing our time and energy in the areas of our lives that we think are most important, and most of us do a horrendous job of that. I think what people can do is to take a real hard look at how those two things line up, and then begin scheduling their time according to what they say their priorities are. Manage their time, not let their time manage them.

I'm not making a value judgment here—I'm not admonishing executives to spend more time at home. What I am saying is to be clear about what you want. Then align that with your actions.

Wright

Yeah, I had a meddlesome yet correct minister tell me yesterday morning that if you want to check your life out, read your checkbook—that's where your priorities are.

Golletz

I'd add the following: You have three types of resources: time, talent, and money. Time is the only one of those three that cannot be replenished. Once it's gone, it's gone! You can always make more money, you can always develop new knowledge, talents, skills, attributes, whatever; but once your time is gone, it's gone forever—you can't get it back. Most of us think of time either as a resource that can be replenished or we don't give it active enough consideration—certainly not the level of consideration we give to our money when we spend it.

Wright

This has been an important conversation. I've really enjoyed talking with you, Rand. I've learned a lot!

Golletz

Thanks very much, David. Let's do it again sometime.

About the Author

After more than twenty years in the corporate world as a Fortune 100 chief marketing officer, director and Practice Leader of the Strategy Consulting Practice for a worldwide, top-ten firm, and as a CEO, Rand Golletz launched his own firm in 2001. It has since set the pace in helping business leaders develop and deploy strength to improve performance.

As a coach, consultant, author, and keynote speaker, Rand's no-nonsense style coupled with his real world, executive experience produces significant results for his clients.

Rand Golletz
Rand Golletz Performance Systems
P.O. Box 5305
Laytonsville, MD 20882
301.482.2598
rand@randgolletz.com
www.randgolletz.com
www.redefiningtypea.com

Chapter Thirteen

An interview with...

Carl Gould

David Wright (Wright)

Today we're talking with Carl Gould. Carl is the founder and director of CMT International, the farthest-reaching business mentoring organization in the world. Carl's innovative approach to business mentoring and business coaching has received acclaim from both his clients and peers. With more than ninety independently owned and operated offices worldwide, Carl Gould and his world-class teams of mentors and coaches have guided their clients to significant results using their proven methods. And they have fun in the process!

Carl, welcome to *Blueprint for Success.*

Gould

Thank you David, I am glad to be here.

Wright

Carl, what is a business and what makes owning a business so enticing?

Gould

David, that is such a great question because there is so much confusion over what a business really is. The dictionary (www.Dictionary.com) defines a business as *"a [profit-seeking] person, partnership, or corporation engaged in commerce, manufacturing, or a service."* The Wikipedia defines a business as *"legally-recognized organizational entity ... designed to sell goods and/or services to consumers, usually in an effort to generate profit."* Can you see why there is confusion? There are so many different and conflicting explanations.

From a practical standpoint, a business is a systematic method of exchanging value. Your company provides a product or service in exchange for currency. Becoming a business owner is enticing for many reasons. Psychologically, a business is a form of self-expression—the vehicle for realizing your dreams. We watch television and read stories of people who have become rich and independent by running their own company. You are no longer answering to "The Man," you are controlling your own destiny with seemingly no constraints. You are calling the shots. You have more time, etc. This is just a partial list.

In the end, David, most entrepreneurs seek freedom and the time to pursue their passions. Launching a business to have more time for yourself is like having children so you can get more sleep! The dream does not have to become a nightmare though. Building a successful business is very simple—not always easy mind you, but simple.

David, there are seven stages that *all* successful businesses encounter. By following the principles of the Success Cycle™, any entrepreneur can realize his or her vision for his or her business.

Wright

What is the Success Cycle™, and how does the Success Cycle™ differ from the lifecycle of a Business?

Gould

The lifecycle tells you where you are *chronologically* in your business life. The Success Cycle doesn't care where you are chronologically, it only cares about how close are you to achieving your measure of success. The Success Cycle is simply a road map. It will illustrate where you are right now relative to where you want to be. By understanding precisely where you are now in the Success Cycle, you can then determine the easiest, quickest, most efficient way to grow your business. We don't favor newness over maturity in a business; it's irrelevant from the standpoint as to whether or not you're going to be successful. Wherever you are in your business life, you can be successful. The Success Cycle maps out precise directions.

By adhering to the 7-Stage method, you will navigate the Success Cycle in an approximate thirty-six-month timeframe. Lifecycles focus on activity, Success Cycles focus on achievement.

Wright

Why do so many independent businesses fail? And why do franchise businesses seem to do so well?

Gould

David, only one out of ten independent businesses will succeed. Nine of ten franchise businesses will succeed. The easy answer is to say that the difference between the two is systems. Franchise businesses have well defined systems. Independent businesses have very little or no systems in place. When you buy a franchise, you are buying the promise of a system, and if followed, that system will make you a millionaire. Systems are the majority of the game David, quite frankly. However, the vulnerability of systems is they are designed for the average person to run them. Owners often rely too heavily on the system itself rather then developing the excellence of the person within that system. This mindset causes mediocrity in a company.

A system on its own can bring you a certain measure of success and at the same time prevent you from reaching your full potential if you have not recruited and developed a winning team. Where most franchise *and* independent businesses falter is that prior to implementing a system, they fail to create an organizational structure. Only one out of ten will thrive because they build a winning "Team" that will implement who's going to do "what" and "with whom." Once you've laid that foundation, you then put in the systems.

When you buy a franchise, the systems are already defined. There still needs to be an infrastructure. To reach your ultimate goal, you must devise the team formation that will work for you. You cannot buy a formation—you must design it on your own. Your team and its culture must be unique to the needs of your operations and the wants of your customers. The franchisor has done part of the work for you by developing the process. That team must then be trained and inspired to excel within that system.

Championship teams have a great system and great players. Mediocre teams lack greatness in one or both of these areas. Conversely, a franchise will fail if you don't follow the system.

David, what most people don't talk about is that most franchises never reach their full potential. Just as purchasing a car doesn't make you a driver, buying a system doesn't make you a successful businessperson. You need to find the right people to do the jobs for which they are naturally suited and then continuously nurture those people. Some franchise owners neglect to put a crew in place internally that will support their systems. They don't have the right people. They lack the leadership that will inspire and motivate their employees to flourish within that system.

Wright

What is the difference between success and failure in running a business?

Gould

Leadership. It's your ability to select the right people, train them, and on a daily basis motivate and inspire them to implement the systems that you have designed for your particular business. Every business is slightly different and requires its own special brand of guidance.

The secret ingredient in business success is the people and their performance. We are surrounded by billions of consumers worldwide and an Internet that connects them all. There is a market for any product. The difference between success and failure in a business is your ability as the owner to impeccably teach your employees their roles and responsibilities so they can in turn reach those consumers with impeccable service. Your willingness to communicate, and to *every day* empower your employees to side with your vision so they go to work enthusiastically to implement that system to create a consistent and enjoyable experience for your customers will determine success or failure in your business.

Wright

Coaching plays a prominent role in the Success Cycle and throughout the 7 Stages. Why is that so?

Gould

David, most people can recognize when they have gotten something wrong or made a mistake. We don't always know when we have gotten something *right*. When we make a mistake, we typically receive immediate and negative feedback. When we get something right, we often second-guess and downplay our triumphs. This habitual pattern leads to the inability to recognize when we have planned and executed successfully.

As an example of this pattern, imagine that you were preparing to sell a real estate property. After researching and consulting subject-matter experts, you decide to market your property for $100,000.

The day comes when the marketing of your $100,000 property goes live. What happens?

The very first person who calls on the property on the very first day of your marketing wants to see the property. Upon entering the property, the buyer proclaims, "I'll take it!" The buyer signs a contract for the full asking price on the spot and then proceeds to take out his checkbook and write you a good faith deposit. The property is sold on the first day of being marketed by the first prospective buyer for the full asking price.

Did you ask the right price or the wrong price for your property?

What was your answer? Did you say the wrong price? Were you wondering if the sale of the house was too easy? Too quick? Not enough resistance or haggling over price by the buyer? Did you begin questioning your asking price? What is going through your mind?

Before we answer this riddle, let's consider a second hypothetical scenario for that same property. After consulting with subject-matter experts and gathering as much information as possible, you decide on a course of action. According to your experts' counsel, it has been determined that you will market your property for $100,000. You have been advised that if you ask that price, you will have the best chance to sell quickly and receive an offer close to your asking price. What happens this time?

The day comes when the marketing of your $100,000 property goes live. What happens?

Day one goes by with no calls, no offers no interest in the property. Then one week . . . one month . . . six months . . . one year . . . three years . . . go by and there are no calls, no offers, and no sale after three years of marketing your $100,000 property.

Did you ask the right price or the wrong price for your property?

What was your answer? Did you say the wrong price? Was this scenario easier to determine? You set a plan in action and it did not yield the result so therefore you asked the wrong price.

In the first scenario, you may have struggled more with your determination of right price versus wrong price. You asked the *right price!* How do we know that you asked the right price? You determined a price target and a time target based on the best information you could gather at the time. After gathering and analyzing that information, you made a decision and executed your plan. You hit the bull's eye! You sold the property at the price you wanted and in the timeframe you desired.

If you struggled with this scenario or are still questioning the logic behind the determination you are not alone. When most people achieve an objective, one of the first things they do is begin to question their result and/or method. This questioning most often leads to doubt their decision-making process. In the case of the example above, you were victorious! Celebrate your accomplishment!

Thinking back on the scenario whereby you sold the property, could there have been areas of improvement? Might you in the future ask a higher price? Not accept the first offer? Of course! You have the benefit of hindsight now. You did not have the benefit of hindsight then. You made the best decision you could given the knowledge you had at the time. Therefore it was the right decision! We can often get blindsided by our rules and social blueprinting. Your coach can see through that conditioning and help you recognize when you get it right!

David, The 7 Stages is a road map. Any driver can benefit from a navigator. When you're making crucial or risky turns, you benefit from somebody who can cover your blind spots. You need a second pair of eyes on the threats and opportunities that you can't see. Your coach is that second pair of eyes. Your coach is someone who is a highly trained, objective, and emotionally neutral professional. His or her main focus is the attainment of your results. Your coach will play a prominent role throughout the course of the 7 Stages because recognizing when you get it 'right' is the accelerator to achievement.

Every successful business has a highly qualified team who implements the owner's vision. According to a New York University study, there is a 72 percent correlation between the value of your business and performance of the people. No longer does the old adage "my balance sheet says I'm good, so I'm good" apply. That is industrial-age entrepreneurship and is no longer the sole measurement of value. Your off-balance sheet intangibles (e.g., people, brand, image, intellectual property, etc.) are what reigns supreme in the new millennium. Value is proportionate to the enjoyment your customers get by interacting with you. Your customers' experience will reflect the attitude of the employees and their leaders. Your coach helps build positive attitude and outlook. Your coaches will build value in your business. Attempting to build a business and navigating the 7 Stages by yourself with no coaches, advisors, or mentors would be akin to entering a beauty pageant and not wearing makeup.

Wright

Carl, would you please take us through a brief description and overview of each of the 7 Stages?

Gould

Certainly David, Picture in your mind, the letter "S." We're going to start at the bottom left-hand corner and work our way upward, beginning with Stage 1.

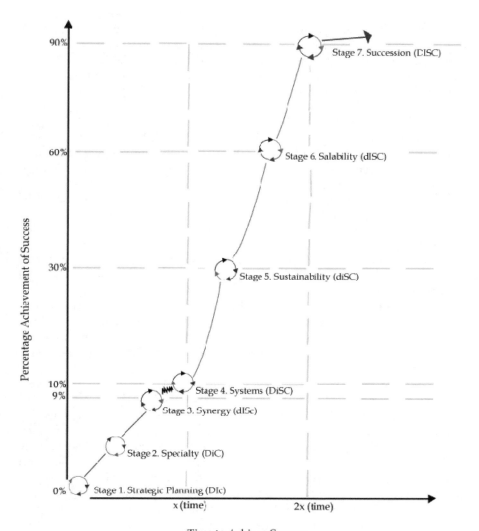

Time to Achieve Success

Stage 1

Stage 1 is the Strategic Planning Stage where your *dream* of owning a business is born. Strategic planning is you designing your dream. You decide you can't work for anyone else—you want to go out and be your own boss. Your dream now needs to get on paper. This is where most business leaders fall down. Emotions often override logic in the entrepreneurial world. Business owners seldom plan properly. Parties and vacations are frequently planned more thoroughly than are most businesses ventures. During Stage 1 you choose the direction of your enterprise, recruit a team, and begin selling your ides to anyone who will listen.

Stage 2

Stage 2 is called the Specialty Stage, where a *job* is born. Even though you launched an idea, you don't have a business yet. You have entered the ranks of the self-employed—you own your job. As long as you, the owner, have to do the work every day, you have a Stage 2 business.

How do you know you have moved beyond Stage 2? Can you leave your business for two months or more and the business will run every bit as good, if not better, when you're gone? If you have to be there every day or the business would fall apart, you're still in Stage 2. Stage 2 is not a bad place to be. If you're a technician, professional, contractor, surgeon, accountant, or attorney, you are a Stage 2 business. You're a "specialist"—self-employed and doing the work.

None of these Stages are good or bad or better than the other, they're just different. As a matter of fact, if you love performing the work yourself, Stage 2 is the place to be. The mission of the 7 Stages is to help you maximize each stage before you go to the next Stage. You can stay your whole career at Stage 2.

Stage 3

Stage 3 is the Synergy Stage, and we say that a *structure* is born. Stage 3 is interesting because often for the first time an owner has to learn how to get along with other people. The owner is faced with and must overcome the demons that have plagued him or her in the past. If the owner does not learn to communicate effectively with others, the business will implode. The business graveyard is littered with Stage 3 businesses that failed to play nice with others. If you are successful in leading others, if you learn "how to play nice in the sandbox" and partner with your employees and vendors alike, you will pass the ultimate test. In growing your business, you avoid this graveyard when you embrace the importance of learning how to train, manage, motivate, and inspire others.

Entrepreneurs are independent by nature. You are a rule-breaker. Stage 3 requires you to instill and to enforce rules. Entrepreneurs frequently take their business to a premature death when they refuse to follow rules. Ironically, the rules they are breaking are their own.

Stage 4

Stage 4 is the Systems Stage. David, a *true business* is born in Stage 4. Now that you have created a team of highly motivated employees, you can now begin implementing the processes and routines that produce a reliable, high-quality experience to the customer. Stage 4 is much like teaching your child how to ride a bicycle. You've pulled the training wheels off and they're pedaling, while white-knuckling the handlebars. You're still running alongside with your hand near the seat in case he or she falls. You are involved, yet your child is pedaling the bike on his or her own. But you do need to stay close. As confidence and competence grows, your child is riding the bicycle forward and not having to look back. You can stop running. You are ready for Stage 5.

Stage 5

Stage 5 is the Sustainability Stage. A *franchise* is born. Whether or not you have purchased a franchise, your business runs without you. Your systems have become the focal point. Your employees have cut the umbilical cord connecting them to you, and the system is running like a finely tuned machine. It is evolving its own personality based on the wants of the customer and the needs of the marketplace. In Stage 1, you worked hard often for unfairly low compensation. When you get to Stage 5, you are unfairly rewarded again on the plus side. You do much less work and you get an incredibly high compensation for it. In Stage 5, you work much less and you are rewarded exponentially high.

The reward for building an infrastructure and implementing a system is that you can launch a new product or division, open multiple locations, and otherwise increase the footprint of your business. You can expand!

Many individual franchise locations will fail to reach their full potential Just because you purchased a franchise, it does not mean you have a Stage 5 business. Many individual franchise locations will fail to reach their full potential. You still need to follow *all* of the steps outlined in the 7 Stages. You have purchased a proven system. That is the good news. The "bad" news is that you will only reach the full potential of the business if you invest the time to plan (Stage 1), learn and master the inner workings of your business (Stage 2), build a team structure (Stage 3), and then mold the systems to reflect the needs of your local culture (Stage 4). You can't *buy* your way to Stage 5 and reach your full potential. You must earn your way to Stage 5 (if you wish to maximize that stage).

Stage 6

Stage 6 is the Salability Stage, and at this stage, an *asset* is born. The business structure and system has value in and of itself. It's now like a piece of real estate. It's now like a collectible item. It's now like a rare coin. Investors will pursue your asset. Your business has become attractive to investors because it is cash flow positive on a regular basis. You've recruited top management. Even if you don't want to sell, salability should be one of the goals for your future. When you have a business that's salable, you are investor-friendly and credit-worthy. Once these milestones are achieved, you have maximized Stage 6.

Stage 7

Stage 7 is the Succession Stage where a *legacy* is born. Many entrepreneurs get into business because they say, "I want to have my own business. I want to be my own boss. I want to be able to retire some day. I want financial freedom. I want to go to the beach, travel, or spend time with my kids." If any of these desires resonate with you, then you need to target Stage 7. The Succession Stage signifies that you can pass along this business to any other entity. You can donate it to a charity, you can sell it, or you can will it to the next generation. You will be awarding them an ongoing asset that generates income monthly whether you are there or not. As a matter of fact, you know you're a State 7 business because you have completed the most significant firing in the history of the business. You've just fired *you!* You've just fired you from the position of CEO, and you have inserted a professional manager in that position. Now, your responsibility is to watch your baby that you've grown from Stage 1 now to Stage 7, flourish on its own. You are now the benefactor of the organization.

Wright

Entrepreneurs are a very independent sort. Can entrepreneurs survive and succeed on their own?

Gould

No. You must succeed using a team because no one person can be all things to all people. Most entrepreneurs think they are, and they will act as if they are, but they're not. And this is where many entrepreneurs run into trouble. You must build your business as a team. You need to have a team of subject-matter experts protect your blind spots because those are the areas that leave you susceptible to attack.

When you're growing a team, David, you must surround yourself with team members who have expertise in areas you do not. If you are a specialist when you walk into a room, you'd better be the smartest person in the room. A lot of specialists who are technically savvy start businesses, and they're the smartest person in the room. As an owner, you need to be a specialist. To be successful as a business owner, you need to be the dumbest person in the room, surrounded by people who are much smarter than you are. In other words, they have expertise in areas that you don't. Even though one person can't be all things to all people, your business "as a team" must be all things to all of your customers. That is why you can't do it on your own and you have to engage and build a team.

Wright

Can any person be successful in growing a business?

Gould

David, the personality of the business will mirror the personality of its owner. There is no one personality type that's better than another. Personality and performance have no correlation. Any personality type can succeed in growing a business. The people who are successful in business embrace their strengths and delegate the rest to others who have strength in areas they don't. That is what makes a successful business. As the leader of an organization, you must accept yourself for what you are and what you are not. Highlight your strengths and have your top advisors protect your blind spots with their strengths.

Wright

Some people reading this right now are considering starting a business. What would your advice be?

Gould

The first thing I would suggest David, is to celebrate. You have made a life-changing decision. Acknowledge yourself for the courageous step you are about to take. Then, get a good night's sleep. Once launched, you may not sleep for a while or want to eat, so do it now! Go out and enjoy. Life is short; eat your dessert first!

Now that you have celebrated, it is time to clean the slate, burn the bridges of your past failures, and blaze forward. The enterprise that you are about to undertake is probably not your first, nor will it be your last. You may have had failures in the past. Remember that regardless of your past history, this endeavor can be successful *if* (I really mean *when*) you follow the 7 Stages. Accept that you may need to change some of your past habitual patterns, and begin modeling the habitual patterns of success.

Your journey begins with Stage 1. You must draft your dream on paper. Understand that growing a successful business can often times feel uncomfortable. It is imperative that on this go-round, you must judge by the results you get and not by the comfort or discomfort you feel along the way. Most entrepreneurs launch a new business in the hopes that ownership will lead to some measure of comfort. The reality of victory is that it comes with a cost. Accomplishment, like many worthwhile events in life, can be difficult. Although this may seem counterintuitive, the more painful it feels in the moment, the better it is working. Your written plan will keep you on track when matters get unnerving.

Once you have your blueprint in writing, you then share your vision. You share your vision with other subject-matter experts (e.g., accountant, attorney, banker, business advisor, etc.) who can point you in the direction you need to go.

Launching a business is a very simple process, David. Celebrate, plan it, and then share your vision with as many people as possible. Those are the three main ingredients for success; and the 7 Stages will guide you throughout that journey.

Wright

Some of our readers are currently struggling in running their small businesses and experiencing frustration, stress, and a *lack* of success. Can they turn it around, and if so, how?

Gould

Yes, it is possible. Turning around a business is much like starting over. All the things we have discussed to this point can also apply to a turn-around situation. In many cases, David, the fact that you're running a business already gives you a head start. You need to first identify the successes to date in your existing business. You will build on those victories. In life as in business, you get what you focus on. If you concentrate your efforts on avoiding past failures, you get more failures. Channel your thought and energy toward success, and that is precisely what you get. Just as you cannot construct a building on a weak foundation, you cannot build a business by attempting to avoid failures.

The Success Cycle is predicated upon developing your strengths and protecting your blind spots. In turning around your struggling business, we focus on the road ahead. In some regards, turning around an existing business can be easier then starting a new one. You have to make some tough decisions as an entrepreneur.

The main distinction you need to recognize is that you cannot take everyone with you. Think of your business as life in a fish bowl. The water inside the fish bowl is your organization. The fish inside are the people in your company. Your business might not be as successful as it can be because the water is too muddy. You need to clean the water. In order to clean up the water, you're going to find that you have a number of fish that thrive in *muddy* water. As you clean the water, you will expose the muddy-water fish. Those muddy-water fish are going to feel "outed." These muddy-water fish will either sabotage your turnaround efforts or they will quit. You must facilitate their exit from the business. If they do not de-select themselves from the new organizational culture (i.e., the clean water), you as the leader need to find them a new role within the company that supports and aligns with their strengths or you need to encourage them to find a job at another company that drinks muddy water. You can't take everybody with you. It is not the people you hire who create a problem in your business, it is the people you are reluctant to fire, even though you know they have worn out their welcome, that drain you.

In the new reality of your business, you will be swimming in cleaner waters. You're going to a new level in your business, you're going to clean up the water, and there is little place for muddy-water fish in your future. Muddy-water fish need to be inserted very strategically and monitored very closely in your organization. Muddy-water fish are one of the biggest blind spots to an entrepreneur. Because you, the entrepreneur, are also a muddy-water fish, it would be very hard for you to recognize the damage they could potentially be doing (and are doing) to your organization, thus the need for your emotionally neutral board of advisors.

It is one of the hardest realizations for owners to make that they cannot drag their employees across the finish line. To the contrary, as an owner you need to make sure you have the right people in the right jobs doing the right work and supporting the future of the business. Your employees need to carry *you* across the finish line. If this is not the case in your company, you will fall victim to the same level of stress and lack of success you had in the past. You can't take everyone with you. Clean up the water and hire clean-water fish to work in it.

Wright

Can a large company/organization employ the same methods of success that a small business does?

Gould

That's a good question, David, and the answer to that is yes. A large business is simply a collection of small businesses. The common mission, vision, values, and purpose are what bring them together. Most large businesses are a consortium of smaller divisions. The principles of the Success Cycle apply to larger business as well.

Wright

Carl, you have seen thousands of businesses worldwide. What are the common trends and habitual patterns that make a successful business? What do failing businesses share in common?

Gould

That is an interesting question, David, because we mentor and coach thousands of entrepreneurial businesses around the world to help them realize their dreams. There was a study conducted by Cornell University that determined that a third of employees are actually not right for their own job—they don't fit the job they're in. Their personality doesn't fit the personality of their job. Another third of the employees are simply not right for the company. The personality of that employee doesn't match the personality of the industry or the company culture. And fully one-half of all people that you employ are not prepared for your future. You may affiliate with sub-contractors and vendors. You may have alliances with other companies. Those companies need to have a similar set of values and ethics. You need to be sure that they subscribe to a similar message as you. The habitual pattern of failure we see is that entrepreneurs will build their business based on who they like rather than their competence. Serious people take serious actions and achieve serious results. While you may have a culture that promotes fun, your people need to be serious about results. Winning the game of business boils down to the players who are in your organization. If you have the right people who enthusiastically embrace the mission, vision, values, and purpose, you will be successful.

David, another visible pattern of success is the alignment of short-term activities and the long-term vision. Championship organizations regularly monitor and measure their short-term activities to see if they are moving toward their long-term goals.

Wright

Why is the alignment of the employees with the MV²P Planning™ so vital to a company's success?

Gould

In sports, if you are an MVP you are the Most Valuable Player. In business, if you are a MV²P organization, you are wholly aligned in Mission, Vision, Values, and Purpose. When in sync, teams and organizations perform at their highest level. If you have people in your company who are not in alignment, you use up all of your energy internally. This could manifest as arguments, strikes, infighting, and other various unpleasantry. Turmoil drains an organization and leaves nothing for the customer. When you lack alignment, you waste the energy to be a top-level organization. Top-level organizations have agreement from top to bottom. Everyone is rowing the boat in the same direction, at the same time, and they do it joyfully and enthusiastically.

Crucial to your success is gaining consensus with your mission, vision, values, and purpose. If someone is not in alignment with the mission, vision, values, and purpose, that person must go. In the end, what makes a business successful is the alignment of the MV²P. It's not the people—yet. The MV²P comes first, and then you plug the people into your plan.

Once you have outlined the structure, you then can systematize what you have created based on your unique business and how you operate in your market. Even national and international franchise companies need to adjust their systems to meet the local culture.

Once you have accomplished these vital steps, you now have a road map with a team of people who look forward to the journey. Going to work becomes a pleasurable experience for the employee and the customers are the ultimate beneficiaries. Your customers become evangelists of your organization and of your product. They will actually partner with you and help you grow. Therefore, alignment with the MV²P becomes paramount.

Wright

Well, what a great conversation. I've certainly learned a lot. I may start making some changes in my own company here. I really do appreciate all this time you've taken with me, Carl, to answer all these questions. It has been enlightening for me.

Gould

David, it has been my pleasure. My wish for you and all of the entrepreneurs who read this book is a prosperous journey along the Success Cycle. Remember that at whatever stage you are in currently, you can maximize that particular stage both financially and emotionally. Should you choose to, you can proceed to the next stages.

Ultimate success in your business is within your reach. Keep it simple, embrace your strengths, protect your blind spots, and build your team of MVPs. The rewards are countless.

Wright

Today, we've been talking with Carl Gould. We've been talking about the 7 Stages of small business success, a groundbreaking method for growing a small business, from start-up to seven figures in three years or less. Carl has developed this methodology for entrepreneurs and managers alike to take the frustration, stress, and mystery out of running a successful small business. He has identified key patterns to running a successful enterprise and his method helps business owners or entrepreneurs focus on activities that will help them close the gap between where they are now and where they would ultimately like to arrive in their business.

Carl, thank you so much for being with us today on *"Blueprints for Success."*

Gould

Thank you David, I enjoyed it as well.

About the Author

For the past two decades, Carl Gould has served as a coach and mentor to entrepreneurs around the world. An acclaimed author, speaker and advisor to some of the most influential organizations in the world (both small and large), Carl has recognized as the foremost authority on closing the gap between where you are now and where you ultimately wish to end up.

His innovative and dynamic approach to business has created significant results for his client. Carl merges timeless principles of success with leading-edge technologies to accelerate achievement. His proven methodologies are both effective and fun!

What began as a passion to help people from all walks of life has grown into Carl's mission to guide individuals and organizations along their path to success. Carl's Global Business Mentoring Program is the farthest-reaching program of its kind in the world. Carl and his team of advisors have overseen the growth and development of thousands of small to medium sized businesses in over 25 countries on 6 continents. As an award-winning coach, Carl has worked with tens of thousands of individuals transform the quality of their life and their level of personal and professional fulfillment.

Carl Gould
www.carlgould.com
1.973.248.6958

Chapter Fourteen

An interview with...

Bruce Bickel

David Wright (Wright)

Today we're talking with Bruce Bickel. Dr. Bickel is founder and president of Transformational Leadership Group, a company he formed in 2003 to train audiences in character-based leadership—its attitudes, attributes, and actions.

For a person to be successful is it important for one to develop a methodology for making decisions?

Bruce Bickel (Bickel)

Absolutely. There is no greater indication of one's leadership style than how one makes decisions. Often, the manner in which the decision is made is as important as the decision that is made. While people may disagree with the ultimate decision, they are more likely to trust the decision-maker when they understand how the decision was made. Having a decision-making process is critical for success at any level. One of the tests of leadership is the ability to weigh all options and the wisdom to choose the right one. That requires a process not a guess.

My football coach at the Naval Academy would never have thought about sending us into a game without a game plan. Granted, the plan was never sacred—we had to make adjustments as the game progressed—but it was critical that there was a plan at the beginning of the contest.

People who do not have a decision-making methodology will allocate their time according to what lands on their desk; thus, other people's priorities will determine their priorities. As a result, most of the time will be spent with problems rather than opportunities. As I learned at Annapolis, "proper planning prevents poor performance."

There is no more productive time than planning ahead. Studies verify that the more time we spend in advance planning, the less total time is required to complete a given project. The beginning of any plan is to establish an appropriate methodology for making decisions.

Wright

Do you find that some people are afraid to make a decision?

Bickel

Yes I do. People often fear the consequences of their decisions because they do not have a consistent plan to make any decision. Thus they require more study, more information, and more input so that everyone can agree with the decision. Consensus nullifies leadership if it is used as a decision-making tool. Granted, a leader should strive for agreement, conformity, like-mindedness, or collective accord, but a leader must refuse to postpone important decisions if consensus cannot be reached.

Leadership requires quick reactions to the unexpected and the ability to respond to the unplanned. A successful leader must rise above the inertia of inaction. Procrastination wears many masks. Whether caused by laziness, forgetfulness, misplaced priorities, stubbornness, or overwork, fear of making a decision poses a time management problem of the greatest magnitude.

When we vacillate between different courses of action—even on very minor issues—for fear of making a mistake, we must remember that indecision is nearly always the worst mistake we can make. Certainly some decisions require more thought and should not be made hastily. After gaining as much knowledge as possible in the time allotted, the effective decision-maker will make a decision and spend his or her full efforts to making the decision work and stop playing the mental "what if" game of reliving the pros and cons of the alternatives.

People can greatly increase their effectiveness by simply giving themselves a deadline for each decision and doing their best to stick to the plan. A decision without a deadline is a vague wish, not an action plan. A self-imposed deadline can provide an atmosphere for learning decisiveness, the ability to finalize difficult decisions on the basis of the knowledge at hand, and the willingness to live with the consequences. Such an assignment to oneself should not be open-ended. Getting in the habit of stretching the deadlines weakens its effectiveness as a motivation to you but also inflicts a thorn to others.

Wright

What are the implications of excessively delayed decisions?

Bickel

The more lukewarm the leadership, the more immobilizing the results. By "lukewarm" I mean the inability to make a decision when a decision needs to be made. Indecision destroys initiative, kills performance, and crushes morale. Morale is the product of the leader's vision and example. Modeling a decision-making process is one aspect of mentoring that can be observed. Often, more is caught than is taught. A true leader does not have to reply upon force, but on the power of example.

Indecision will cause a "bottleneck" within any organization (even a family) when the person responsible for making the decision fails to take an essential action. This results in time wasted by an entire group of people. It may be the corporate executive who delays saying yes or no to a new idea; the teacher who waits until the last minute before assigning term paper topics; the planning committee that can't decide on details of the silent auction far enough in advance to give the development committee time to acquire auction items; or the husband who delays scheduling vacation time to coincide with the children's return to school. Most people don't realize how much they thwart the efforts of subordinates and co-workers by failing to make decisions in a timely manner. Punctuality applies to decision-making just as much as it does to arriving on time at an event. It shows respect for other people and the limited time that they have.

Wright

Do you have a decision-making tool that you have found successful?

Bickel

Yes I have. I have adopted insights I gained from the Apostle Paul in his letter to the Church at Corinth as he counseled the early church in their decision-making.

Wright

What do you mean?

Bickel

He gives three profound principles of decision-making in the context of the liberties that one has and at the same time establishes the limitations of liberty as a means a creating a balanced decision-making matrix. I have found this matrix to be extremely useful and helpful for about every decision I have to make, either in my personal or my professional life. In essence, it is a blueprint for making decisions. Paul says, "Everything is permissible for me but not everything is beneficial; everything is permissible for me, but I will not be mastered by anything; everything is permissible, but not everything is constructive."

Wright

You refer to his instruction as principles; what are the principles you are referring to?

Bickel

They are the Principle of Personal Progress, the Principle of Personal Authority, and the Principle of Social Relationships. I have found these principles to be most helpful in what I would call the "gray areas of life," those areas in which there is no clear or obvious choice. As responsible citizens we know we must operate within the laws of our land. Those choices are the easy ones because boundaries have already been established. It's in the less obvious areas that we have our most difficulty in making decisions.

Wright

How do you apply these principles when making decisions?

Bickel

Let's take them one by one. The first is the Principle of Personal Progress. Essentially, everything that is not prohibited by law is permissible but not every possibility that exits may be beneficial to me. The figurative idea of the word "beneficial" is that of freedom to make progress upon a pathway. The thing that is beneficial hastens the traveler upon his journey. The Greek word means "to carry together"—to co-operate. Visualize throwing a stick into a flowing stream that is moving in a certain direction. The stick now moves in the direction of the flowing water. That's the idea of this word and thus the word can be translated "profitable."

Of course, one has to be certain that the stream is moving in the right direction to be "profitable." The profitableness of any decision must be tested by "will this decision help me co-operate with my moving in the direction of my mission or calling in life?" One must know oneself well enough to know what will be profitable and what will not. There is no law that says I can't attend a certain movie or read certain magazines, but I have to know myself well enough to know that certain movies or literature may stimulate things within me that will not be profitable for my life's journey. Art is permissible as well as music, science, and recreation, etc.—all are permissible. But some of these things that are permissible are not profitable or beneficial—they will not hasten my personal progress toward the goal of my life. Thus, I ask the question, "Is this something that will be profitable for my personal development?"

Wright

What about the second principle?

Bickel

This is the Principle of Personal Authority. Within the boundaries of the law, I have a myriad of choices that I have the power to choose, but I must not be mastered by any of them. We must test our relationship to all things by this principle. Money is permissible, but I will not be brought under the power of money. Knowledge is permissible, but I will not be a slave to knowledge.

We assert our liberty by recognizing its limitations. One's liberty to use anything perishes when the things we use become our masters and we are enslaved by them. While a particular thing may be permissible (e.g., golf, recreation, hobbies, habits, work, career, friendships, manner of thinking, or passion of living), if these things master me, then have I not lost my liberty? This principle follows logically the first one. We must know our mission—our direction or calling in life—in order to ensure that nothing else becomes our master. When the innocent, legitimate, permissible thing becomes master, it is no longer innocent, it is absolutely illegitimate, and it is unutterably improper.

Wright

The third principle sounds interesting. How do you apply it in your life?

Bickel

The last test is, "not all things are constructive." This is the principle of social relationships. Here again, I see a limitation to my liberty. While I have a multitude of things that I know are permissible, there are some things that, if I take and use, I shall not build up my neighbor by so doing. There are many choices I have the freedom to make, but I must not indulge in any of them without keeping in mind that, along with the necessity for my own personal progress, is the necessity for contributing to the building up of my neighbor's well being.

Wright

How do priorities fit into your decision-making model?

Bickel

Knowing and adhering to one's priorities greatly enhances the effectiveness of decision-making. There are two ways of setting priorities: according to urgency or according to importance. Most people set priorities according to urgency, which is why they spend so much time putting out fires or managing problems.

As a midshipman at the Naval Academy, I read a marvelous little book titled, *The Tyranny of the Urgent*. If I remember correctly, decisions could be grouped in the following categories: Important and Urgent (i.e., must be done immediately or in the near future and take precedence over everything else). Important but not urgent (i.e., these can be done now or later and are the things we never get around to completing).

The important but not urgent things are generally postponed indefinitely unless we initiate a self-imposed timetable to accomplish them. These include such things as: completing the will you know you need to create, the diet you know you need to begin, the book you want to read, the eye examination you need to schedule, and the continuing educational course you must complete fall into this group.

Next, the Urgent but not Important (i.e., these cry out for immediate action, but if examined objectively, would be a low priority). Things that fall into this category include: being asked to attend a meeting, chair a committee, or give a speech at an event. While we might consider them a lower priority, someone is waiting for an answer.

Neither Important nor Urgent is another category. These things are diversionary that provide a feeling of activity and accomplishment, but give an excuse to put off the more difficult important issues. This is known as "busy work" or perhaps "wasted time." Cleaning out one's desk drawers at the office or rearranging files, while giving one a sense of accomplishment, are probably rather low on the priority scale. If we are honest, we have to admit that about 95 percent of all television viewing is wasted time.

We cannot protect our priorities unless we master the most effective time-saving technique ever developed—the decision to say *no*. We must learn to decline, graciously but firmly, every request that does not contribute to our personal progress, those things that will have a tendency to master us, or those that are not constructive to the well being of others. Learning to say no to oneself or to others is a choice in decision-making that must be mastered. A question I ask myself when facing such choices is, "Does this task help or hinder the achievement of my personal progress, gain mastery over me, or not encourage others?" Please see previous description of the three principles to clarify these questions.

Wright

In our complex world, how do you determine your priorities?

Bickel

Here again I rely upon the wisdom of the Apostle Paul, this time in his letter to the Ephesian church. The instruction to his friends in this newly formed fellowship is powerfully practical. The order of priorities outlined by this divinely inspired sage is as applicable today as it was centuries ago: Be a Responsible Person, Be a Responsible Partner, Be a Responsible Parent, Be a Responsible Provider, Be a Responsible Penetrator of the World. The character quality of responsibility—knowing and doing what is expected of me—is key to priority management.

Wright

Is there significance to the order of these priorities?

Bickel

Very definitely. Consider the last priority as the result of living according to the order of the first four. If a person wants to really impact his or her world, one must start with being a responsible person. This is the focal point—the starting point—in impacting the world. It starts with each person being individually responsible. Our culture spends too much time talking about our individual rights and not enough time about our individual responsibilities. Life is not about rights; life is about responsibilities. If we want to have a responsible world, we have to be responsible people.

If married, the foundation for being a responsible partner is being a responsible person. Marriage becomes the arena in which we perfect our person (our character) with our partner. Likewise, being a responsible parent is founded upon being a responsible partner. Parenting is perpetuating your person (character) in your progenies. Being a responsible provider is providing necessary provisions for your family. When we live according to this order of priorities, we will impact the world—we will be a Responsible Penetrator of the World.

Simply stated, although difficult to practice, these priorities are: life, marriage, family, work, and influence. Notice that influence is the result, not the cause, of one's priorities. This order applies to unmarried people also, but in the order of life, work, and influence. I must point out that once married, work drops a level, and once the family is expanded with children, work drops another notch. In my counseling, I tell singles that if they want to have work control their lives, don't get married and have children.

Wright

Please summarize your thoughts on decision-making.

Bickel

Decision-making is a function of character and it begins with how one thinks. Thoughts become our words and words become our actions. Actions become our habits and habits become our character. Character becomes our destiny.

I encourage people to make a Character Covenant with themselves—making an arrangement with oneself to serve as a grid to regulate one's conduct and decision-making process. Ask: Will this decision help me cooperate with my life's calling? Will this decision gain inappropriate mastery over me? Will this decision hinder the development of others? Making a Character Covenant is a good place to start.

About the Author

DR. BRUCE BICKEL is president and founder of Transformational Leadership Group, LLC, and Senior Vice President and Managing Director of Private Foundation Management Services, PNC Wealth Management, Pittsburgh, Pennsylvania. Bruce graduated from the United States Naval Academy in 1966 with a BS in Electrical Engineering. After serving in Southeast Asia in an aviation capacity, he served as Vice President of the Fellowship of Christian Athletes. Bruce addresses issues concerning character and ethics as related to organizational effectiveness.

Bruce Bickel
Transformational Leadership Group, LLC
P.O. Box 24567
Pittsburgh, PA 15234
Phone: 412.389.1315
E-mail: usna1966@verizon.net